Walking To Know

Walking To Know

A Meditation on Place
Considering the Design Legacy of the Camino de Santiago

Germán T. Cruz

Library of Congress Control Number: 2012907695
ISBN: Hardcover   978-1-4771-0498-9
        Softcover   978-1-4771-0497-2
        Ebook   978-1-4771-0499-6

This book was printed in the United States of America.

To order additional copies of this book, contact:
Xlibris Corporation
1-888-795-4274
www.Xlibris.com
Orders@Xlibris.com
113771

CONTENTS

Part One

Pilgrimage and Memory

Reflexions and Lessons on the Way to See and to Know

In the Manner of Introduction

This book relates an adventure long in planning and relatively short in execution. The appeal of a 1,000 mile walk on the Camino de Santiago began to tickle my imagination about 10 years ago after reading some travelogues and investigating the historical background and impact of the route and the pilgrimage. Soon, I began to see the quest as an adventure of mind, body and spirit with numerous opportunities for application to an understanding of landscape and community. Additional research and dialogue greatly expanded my understanding and tempted me to become spiderlike by throwing linkages in every direction and create a web of reasons, connections, and motivations for a 66 day walk across a continent. Over time, I became sort of a Templar Knight or a Cistercian monk delighting in ancient tales and anecdotes along with the historical context of 10 centuries. Eventually I began to see rather than look at the underside of the tradition and became more convinced of the need to walk and see or better yet, to walk in order to see. My enthusiasm convinced my wife to be a partner in adventure and we began to plan on paper a real adventure on the land and the cultures. Finally, we found the time, secured funding from our own resources, entrusted our home and cat to a caretaker, and took off for the point of beginning at the southeastern corner of France in Le Puy en Velay. To that point everything was quite simple and under control. What followed was a delightful adventure across land and culture that has transformed our entire being (mind/body/spirit) and given us a larger sensitivity for land, people, and culture.

Thus, this book represents a meditation or reflection on the pilgrimage tinted with a scholarly lens and a travelogue commentary on places and events during the pilgrimage. The use of the word "pilgrimage" denotes the nature of the journey beyond mere physical effort and near an extraordinary spiritual and mental enterprise. There was no search for "enlightenment" as much as a sincere desire to know and to see. To know the places and to see the land close up. To partake of the experience of thousands of other "pilgrims" across 10 centuries. For organizational purposes the book consists of two major sections that complement one another and serve to clarify and amplify both text and testimony. Section One addresses issues of design interest in a holistic rather than a technical manner while Section Two presents a narrative of the experience that serves to place the journey in focus. The symbiotic engagement between the two sections results in a richer narrative of causality that affirms purpose and consequence of journey. Many conclusions are left to the reader and no strict delimitation is made of the discussion boundaries except for the centrality of truth and the guiding power of passion. Without a doubt, this book is about open and truthful personal quests and does not conform to overriding socio-political frameworks of dialogue. As shown in the bibliography (pages 81-85), many works of varied provenance were consulted and care was exercised to emphasized salient and outstanding concepts and ideas with bearing on the quest. The intention was not to produce a treatise (ie: "Complutensian Polyglot") but rather to express an experience and its consequences upon a person, a mind, and a spirit.

Hakuna Matata! What a wonderful phrase

Hakuna Matata! Ain't no passing craze

It means no worries for the rest of your days

It's our problem-free philosophy

Hakuna Matata!

Music by Elton John, Lyrics by Tim Rice

A journey of this dimension is only made possible by the assistance of many people. Above all, a large expression of gratitude post-mortem is given to Robert and Grace Kenyon along with Marybelle Coate whose legacy enabled travel. Within the circle of gratitude (hakuna matata!!) stand tall in heart and memory several good people: Kim Coe who housesat and cat minded during our absence; Debbie Schink who guarded our hearts and home with boundless energy and affection; Dr. Azucena Cruz who challenged our minds (and bodies) with pertinent phenomenological commentary and references; sixty-six gite, refuge, and hostal keepers who provided clean restful places, laundry services (often with dryers), and some excellent meals; many bartenders and waitresses that gave directions to places and information to enlarge the experience; more than one hundred pilgrims who shared portions of the walk and evenings of conversation; farmers and city dwellers who fed our thirst and curiosity; writers of guidebooks that helped plan the journey and find places of note; various friends and family who were amazed at our insanity and nevertheless kept us in mind and prayer. To all, Thank You, very much.

Other Pilgrimage Routes

Several countries have historical routes that serve as pilgrimage circuits representative of culture and faith. The following is a non-comprehensive sample of some major routes:

In Japan, the route of the eighty-eight temples in the island of Shikoku represents a classic Japanese Buddhist pilgrimage that extends for 1300 kilometers across challenging terrain and has tested pilgrims over a thousand years. A test of body and spirit that opens the mind to a total experience of renewal.

In India, The Char Dham ("four abodes") pilgrimage circuit in the Indian Himalayas connects four important temples in Indian Buddhism (Puri, Rameshwaram, Dwarka, and Badrinat) located in the Garwhal section of the state of Uttaranchal (formerly the northwestern section of Uttar Pradesh). The four sites represent the four cardinal points of the Indian sub-continent and were grouped by the philosopher Shankaracharya (Adi Sankara) in the 8th century. Each site in the circuit has an autonomous history and significance that predates and remains distinct from their status as a circuit; however, inclusion in the Char Dham has, over time, caused them to be viewed together in popular imagination and actual pilgrimage practice.

A Sunday Walk Enlarged

Walking across the land from mountain to mountain or river to river is certainly not a new activity although is far from a Sunday stroll in the park. Homo erectus and its antecedents and successors covered great distances across continents carving out paths for migration and hunting that might have also served as routes of pilgrimage and discovery. Human history has been written on foot across the land only to be recorded later in calligraphic finger steps upon parchment or paper. Mankind is united and defined across the centuries by single steps taken by the desire to reach beyond, to understand the land in its entirety, to observe and compare differences and also very much to conquer, barter, control and subjugate. The steps of free men and slaves, male and female, dark and light of skin are marked not only in distances but also in cultural legacies and exchanges. The sense of time and space derived from marches and walks of various dimensions and purposes expanded the understanding of place. By place it is understood the location of person and community particular to a group of individuals. Boundaries of place vary in size and scale. This pedestrian (foot driven) understanding enabled mankind to achieve a deeper as well as a more particular awareness of various relationships in the sciences and the arts that made for a greater definition of the qualities and resources of places. Consequently, a better usage of the environment arose to support what can best be called an eco-balanced existence long before there were "green" policies and "environmentalism" driven efforts. A consilient view of Man and Nature ran congruent with the pilgrimage route to bring about improvements in agricultural irrigation, potable water supply networks, farming practices, civic unity, as well as governance. Despite warfare by alien interests (Albigensian Crusade, 100 Year War, Wars of Religion, Jewish and Moorish Expulsion, etc) the communties along the pilgrimage routes existed in relative peace with one another and managed to retain their character and integrity. By merely walking, men absorbed the meaning and value of place and established an exchange value for their transit. This exchange of monetary and cultural value continues to these days. The emergence of local character eventually gave rise to regional awareness which in turn fed national identities even to the creation of nation states.

The feet of long distance walkers and travelers became then and today the carriers and purveyors of knowledge. In essence, we are

In South America, the Inca road system (called Capaq Ñan or Gran Ruta Inca) connected the Inca Empire with an estimated network of 40,000 kilometers designed for use in all kinds of climate and intended to move people, mail, and goods as well as armies across the length and breadth of the empire. From Tumbes (Peru) to Talca (Chile), and between Quito (Ecuador) and Mendoza (Argentina), the road crossed deserts and Andean Highlands to establish a netwrok that united the empire both politically as well as physically and spiritually. Some sections were paved with cobblestones while others were just tamped dirt pathways between 3 to 12 feet wide. In response to the terrain, the Inca built causeways, stairs, river crossings, tunnels, retaining walls and switchbacks along with rest stations (tampu) at 22 to 26 km intervals that provided lodging, food, and supplies. Relay runners called chasqui stationed along the road at 1.4 km intervals carried Information along the road either verbally or stored in quipu (accounting and message device of multicolored knots). In special circumstances, exotic goods could be carried by the chasqui: it was reported that Sapa Inca at Cusco (capital of the empire) could dine on 2 day old fish from the coast, a travel rate of 240 km a day by relay runners.

podriatic consequences. Places were reached on foot, explored, analyzed and categorized in terms of commerce, settlement, botanical and mineral value as well as religion and esoteric meanings. Thus, Northern dwellers in the plains of North America exchanged goods and rituals with natives of Meso-America in similar fashion as the walk to China by the Polos of Venice that enriched aspects of European civilization in ways above and beyond a silk exchange or noodle making techniques. By walking in long set march routes the Incas connected their empire in much the same way that Europe became a larger continent along the various routes of pilgrimage or Japan was united in staged journeys between Buddhist temples during the Samurai era. By walking to Santiago de Compostela in NW Spain pilgrims from Geneva, Le Puy, Oslo, Brussels, Aix-la-Chapelle, Berlin, Paris, Tours, Prague, Turin, Budapest, Zagreb, Venice, Bari, Naples, Arles, Barcelona, Madrid, Granada, Seville, and Lisbon established networks of refuges, markets, and walking routes that became intrinsic to commerce and culture. The pilgrimage routes became the main streets of the continent long before autobahns and national highways came into the scene. This network of walking routes became in effect the structural armature for the European Union with additional linkages to eastern Europe and Asia Minor. It is then possible to view the concept of European Union as a continent bound by blood through wars and by faith through steps of pilgrimage with commerce and culture generously placed in between.

Whether long or short, marches across land have defined territories (regions or nations) in both physical and ideal ways. The physical is a human dimension while the ideal is a mental space. The boundaries of a small city on the banks of the Tiber expanded to central England and Asia Minor by foot on a web of roads that enabled a larger projection of itself as well as the injection of culture and goods into itself. The city of Rome grew from its small town origins in the 8th century BC to become the center of a large empire not only in measurable distances but also in cultural and political dimensions. The "idea" of Rome has survived as an exemplar of governance (Republic) and culture far beyond the historical boundaries. The physical dimension grew upon a well developed and maintained network of 53,000 miles of "Roman roads" that connected the empire and welcomed travel by armies; as well as, scholars, merchants, vagabonds, poets, philosophers, evangelists, prisoners of war, farmers, produce peddlers, barbarian invaders, and a variety of cultures that expanded the original city context beyond the banks of the Tiber River. These roads (8 to 10 feet wide with soft shoulders) were in fact the first "internet" network of Europe. The roads were not only a defense/access network but also a commerce and culture causeway. In the first century of the Common Era, it was possible for a letter, a book or a bolt of cloth to reach Rome from Alexandria, London or Tripoli is one week's time. Today

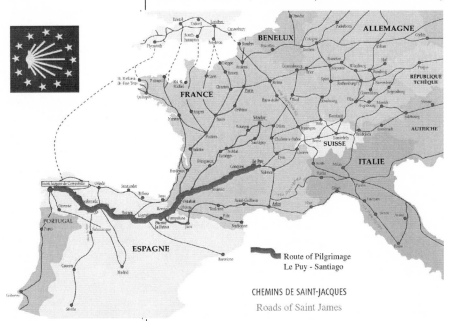

CHEMINS DE SAINT-JACQUES
Roads of Saint James

Routes of the Camino de Santiago in Europe

Source: European Union/ Directorate General for Education and Culture

Marco Polo (1254 - 1324) authored **Il Milione** (Travels of Marco Polo) telling the story of his walk and life in China under Kublai Khan

we marvel at the speed with which Amazon and other merchants can deliver goods in one or two days between and within Europe and America. It is hard to imagine how such high speed of delivery was possible in an era without the benefit of telephones, internet, and high speed transportation by land and air. Distance and time have been shrunk in our times; however, the physical extension of the land remains. From St. Jean Pied du Port to Santiago the physical distances have not changed and the walking capacity of pilgrims is no higher or faster today than those of 400 or 800 years past. Humans still walk at 4km per hour with ocassional dashes to 6km per hour but topography and human endurance impose limits that are hard to overcome. Aside from distance and speed, the road networks demanded the acquisition and exchange of knowledge along with the practice of currency exchange, lodging and feeding strangers (banking and hostelry). Eventually, anti-social forces emerged and it was necessary to introduce protection (chivalry and monastic armies) to ensure safe travel by all pilgrims. Just like a pebble falling on a lake surface creates a ripple effect, the pilgrimage routes across the world have fostered ancillary developments that gave rise to contemporary practices duly modified to accomodate local needs. On a more formal level, the pilgrimage routes influenced the location and form of towns as much as contemporary roads have had a decided impact upon urban form and function. It is worth noting that cities along the Roman road network experienced significant "sprawl" quite similar to current conditions.

Charlotte Harris Rees. **Secret Maps of the Ancient World.** AuthorHouse. 2008

In the general talk about places and routes of exploration or pilgrimage, there is need for acknowledgement of mapping and their role in describing place while also providing guidance. Map makers were decisive participants in the creation and identification of places. A map maker by the name Vespucci legated his first name (Amerigo) to the newly discovered world in the 15th century. Dutch map makers created exquisite works of navigation and location richly illustrated with images of a world to be known. A land beyond, depicted with imagination that sought to answer the curiosity of horizon observers from the piers of Spain and Portugal as well as Amsterdam. Even in our times we have become aware of ancients maps that seem to portent a Chinese presence in America before Columbus (Charlote Harris Rees).

A remarkable replication of the Roman road system is the current network of national roads and interstate highways that crisscross the continental USA, enabling the movement of goods and people as well as the exchange or affirmation of regional cultures. Walking between refuges ("gites") or from convent to convent has been replaced by driving across longer distances between homes and motels. For the past 60 to 70 years swarms of silver Airstream cocoons have migrated from campground to campground across the continent creating portable villages and transporting culture across the land while extending the spiritual dimension of an American pilgrimage by diverse routes to access Nature and experience "re-creation" across shortened distances and times. In this swarming of the continent a fresh concept of country and a deeper understanding of land has emerged. Places once remote or unaccessible are now part of the daily perceptive experience of both the North-American continental culture as well as the world awareness. This phenomena is noteworthy for its compressive impact upon perception and culture. The reduction of distances by increased speed of travel has the adverse consequence of removing details from the perceptive range. Movement and circulation act as change elements in perception to the loss of detail and understanding not unlike the work on logistics of perception by Paul Virilio and others. Yet, there is a core of identity that remains and undergirds transformations. The task of new pilgrims then becomes both anthropological and archeological in search for the autochthonous reality of places.

The great American western migration in the 19th century unveiled not only land and resources but also cultures both local and foreign. A new awareness of dimension and distance emerged that was different from a mere scenic or aesthetic pleasurable experience in the "country". Moreover, the influx of people (pilgrims) into the West caused a renewed dialogue with land and resources that directed settlement patterns and agricultural/industrial practices to essentially redefine the land. In many ways, the redefined character of the new lands motivated new expressions in art and literature as well as folklore ("Oklahoma"/Aaron Copland/"The Music Man"/Martha Graham/Rodeo) beyond the obvious sociological/psychological rubrics. Topography and natural resources promoted deeper study along with regional asessment tools (GIS/Photogrammetry/Aerial Photography/Satellite Imagery) that have in turn advanced further study and more detailed analysis. This flux demands clarity, as well as, well drawn pespective linkages. Recently (September 2010), at the final stage of the competition for design of the Seattle Central Waterfront, James Corner leading the presentation by The Field Operations Team offered a compelling illustration of the manner in which he as a non-native (a pilgrim) had come to undertand the land context and extent of the country that enabled a clearer vision of the Pacific coast. From a series of aerial photographs of land between East and West coasts (by Alex S. McClean) he offered a learning experience to be used profitably in the local design context. This vision was deeply contextual rather than merely anecdotal and offered greater linkages of significance for what could ultimately be seen as larger than a 9 acre impact of a highway crossing a city. Thus, Corner related the project to the nation and the territory, along with its attributes both human and physical, demonstrating capacity for design to create a "transformative space" with contextual awareness, innovative thinking and effective public engagement (bonhommie as Aristotle would call it in his listing of civic virtues). Corner's team won the assignment and it is quite sure that other teams of designers will imitate this presentation in pursuit of other projects of equal or lesser dimension. The problem is that none of them would have had a parallel or similar pilgrimage. The old adage

Paul Virilio. *Negative Horizon: An Essay in Dromoscopy.* Continuum. London. 2005
_____. *A Landscape of Events*. MIT Press. Cambridge. 2000
_____. *Lost Dimension*. Semiotext(e). New York. 1991
_____. *War and Cinema: The Logistics of Perception.* Verso. London. 1989
_____. *Speed and Politics: An Essay on Dromology.* Semiotext(e). New York. 1977/1986

James Corner/Field Operations presentation on the Seattle Waterfront design competition as well as those of the other teams can be seen in:
www.cityofseattle.net/transportattion/waterfront_design.htm

of walking a mile in someone else's shoes applies to design action as well as to journeys in life or land.

Within this discussion of context, a consideration of scale is worth noting. The villages and hamlets that grew out of the pilgrimage routes have eventually become larger entities that now embrace territories and even small countries. Territoriality as a quality of place becomes a concern within concepts of distance and time. How big is a territory? The old way of dimensioning land reflected a journey (one day travel) between edges. The current times have increased the dimension by reason of speed and means of travel beyond mere walking from about 32 km (about 20 miles) to 588 km (about 480 miles) by automobile at 60mph. Here lies a great conflict with absorption of information and detail, since at higher speeds of travel the context tends to blur and dissipate both in visual perception and mental acknowledgement. The difference is now between a mixture where particles are distinguishable to a blend where all particles lose identity in favor of new colors and textures, radically removed from their original character. Thus, the question arises: How can a contemporary walking action be used to achieve a better and clearer view and understanding of the reality of land planning and use? Is there a better measure for 21st century pilgrims? Can the steps on land be correlated with steps in space? Do Amstrong's footprints on the moon correlate with human steps in an earthly pilgrimage route? It might well be that from walking under the Milky Way, man can now dream of walking on the Milky Way in a sidereal pilgrimage. Along the Camino there is the overhead comforting presence of the Milky Way as a canopy of the infinite guiding the way. What would be the new guiding canopy in outer space?

The following pages represent a testimony or a manner of seeing derived from personal experience. It is neither entirely new nor normative. It is simply the personal view of someone with almost half a century of experience and some restless spirit of inquiry. Like fingerprints, every step is unique and speaks of a correspondIngly unique experience. As such, it is only original as it represents the evolution of an ethic of engagement and discovery rather than a programmed journey into foreordained unknown areas of the disciplinary galaxy. The intent is humane rather than strictly scholarly or pedantic (narrow, often ostenta tious concern for book learning and formal rules). The humane demands an engagement with humans in all their complexity rather than just with the neutral

Alex MacClean. **Designs on the Land: Exploring America from the Air.** Thames and Hudson. 2003. With an introduction by James Corner.

Alice Foxley. **Distance and Engagement: Walking, Thinking and Making Landscape**. Vogt Landscape Architects. Lars Müller Publishers. Baden. 2010

Rutheford Platt. **The Humane Metropolis**. Lincoln Institute. 2006

George Hargreaves. **Landscape Alchemy**. ORO. 2009

Edward S. Casey. **Earth-Mapping: Artists Reshaping Landscape**. Minnesota. 2005

"landscape" and selected inanimate objects of heartfelt concern. An engagement of one shared with others that is vastly more real and demands greater perspicuity and more focused imagination. Professionals like Günther Vogt have rooted their practice upon a deep engagement with the land by walking and an awareness of humanity by inclusion, while geographers like Rutherford H. Platt advocate for a comprehensive approach that includes all systems natural and human very much in the manner of several previous designers and geographers like Ian McHarg and M.R. G. Conzen. Per Marc Treib (*The Content of Landscape*), the work of George Hargreaves can also be included in this group. Hargreaves book title (*Landscape Alchemy*) superimposes two ancient concepts that harken to a connectivity between land and experimentation that is at the core of a humane approach. Further upfield, Edward Casey (*Earth Mapping*) sees a reshaping of landscape by artists "mapping" the land in response to various stimuli, needs, and perceptions. In many ways this is akin to the efforts of mapmakers in the 15th and 16th century to apply imagination rather than exactitude to the representation of newly discovered places and peoples. In our age, the mapping of places is more physically correct but it might not be truly exact in our perception for lack of imagination in the same manner that drawing with digital software through a laser printer is not quite the same as hand etching by Rembrandt van Rijn (1606 - 1669) or Johannes Vermeer (1632 - 1675) on a copper plate. Somehow, the human trace (*humana imaginen*) is absent in the sharp and technically perfect work of laser printing free from the recombinant presence of DNA. These pages will bear witness to such differences. Undoubtedly, some will disagree and take issue with any or all of the issues touched in these pages. Their voices are welcomed with grace and interest. Not all monks had a perfect voice for Gregorian chanting and the imperfect chants were directed beyond human ears and above the choir loft to a larger entity. Consonance and disonance allow for human error or diversity. Correction is welcomed to make the chanting better, but will not necessarily make it as perfect as the composition on paper (parchment) might suggest.

Pilgrimage

Design can aptly be likened to a pilgrimage and the designer to a pilgrim. Upon this act of faith (confidence in competence) can be placed the mission and action of engagement with the natural and built world to effect tranformations of benefit to people and places. Theoretical and practical roads and pathways traced by the physical design disciplines blend with existing networks and systems to create a complex of connections and causeways representative of human and cultural presence over time. More than a mere spiritual or a technical competence exercise, the design pilgrimage extends across mind, body and spirit to engage the total person in such manner that the pilgrim labors in direct contact and tension with the ground (land) and the environment (landscape) across a multi-dimensional scenario, while seeking a clearer understanding of direction and purpose in actual time and place. It might be argued that a process of **progressive revelation** takes place in the design pilgrimage that enlightens the journey toward the attainment of clarity and order. In contemporary terms the pilgrimage must be conducted in context with the natural as well as the supernatural and the intranatural. Of course, this multi-natural path challenges a multitude of fashions and opinions about the procedure and outcome of design action. Among them is the supposition that designers need to be neutral and produce corresponding neutral outcomes which meaning will be determined by user groups or well thinking critics. The response to this has been a proliferation of form driven outcomes imbued with sameness that is far from a much vaunted "universality" anchored in a "diversity" dominant view. Regretfully, it seems like each successful or noteworthy design solution triggers a fever of formal imitation that eventually falls into a cacophony of forms and masses with little meaning and no discernible voice tone. The Vietnam Memorial by Maya Lin has been reproduced in various forms and with various materials from sea to shining sea while loaded with an excess of emotion that passes for true concern and impact. The carefully conceived and strongly contextual geometric (modernistic) solutions by Dan Kiley have been imposed upon myriad of sites by designers of all stripes bereft of creativity and research rigor. The infrastructure and form work of European designers like Gilles Clément, Adrian Gauze, Michel Corajoud and Allain Provost emerges in spiritless copies or imitations taken from the latest books or magazines by "designers" poor in inspiration or courage. The minimalist work of Peter Walker is used for "inspiration" by practitioners and students

Progressive revelation argues for a basic operational background extensively tested and demonstrable true (reiterative recombination) that is enriched by fresh understandings and localized stimuli. The reiterative recombination used in synthetic biology for DNA construction provides a rich emulative opportunity for multi-facetic progressive engagements of design with place. This progressivity contrasts with static operational modes anchored in a fixed set of dogmas and practices with no proven current value or legitimacy. The ethical concept of progressivity relates to a view of landscape as a dynamic system rather than a stationary organism independent of its locus. Awareness of background and foreground are important considerations for understanding of the middleground.

Formality and the locus of place has been addressed quite extensively in regard to landscape and design. See Marc Treib. **The Content of Landscape Form** (*The Limits of Formalism*). Landscape Journal. January 1, 2001. for example.

eager to use form as a convenient solution to their sterility within a senseless pursuit of fashionability. In all, the humane and its research demands are forsaken while the sterile and the mechanical are trapped in available form "exemplars" that are celebrated as wonderful expressions of modernity or contemporaneity. In this respect, form is certainly easier to emulate and imitate than reason and inspiration. Yet form by itself needs the strong support of directed inquiry as much as triangles need theorems. Marc Treib and others have sought to inform and challenge mere form driven exercises in relation to a humane (natural) rather than a formalized (geometric) place outcome: *I would propose that we continue to seek a landscape architecture that engages more fully aspects of human and natural presence, as well as human and natural histories, poetically elevating them through formal dexterity. To provide drainage or seating is only the first response; then one can make that canal or bench beautiful in itself and, perhaps more importantly, an integral contributor, if not instigator,for the greater scheme. As Edward Weston once said: "Photograph a thing not for what it is, but for what else it is." (The Limits of Formalism).* The power of geometry (form) to fool the eye and the mind is then well recognized along with a dire need for a more autochthonous (formed or originating in the place where found) expression that reflects the human condition in true reality rather than as an intellectually convenient or situational ethical construct. Here the need for a clear ethic can be probably best identified more in the traditional concept of good/beautiful/true (Aquinas et alii) free from legalistic or antinomian frameworks. Of necessity, the design pilgrimage must transit and resolve these conflicts with integrity rather than earnest or heartfelt sentimentality. The assumed "stewardship of Nature" cannot be extended to idolatry along with support for anything or anybody that purports to "save" or "protect" Nature as if it were a creature in a zoological park or a porcelain figurine in a shelf. Nature contains us and a proper "preservation" must of necessity include us. Stewardship is more akin to guiding support than control and enslavement or enshrinement. Truly, Nature is too vast and complex for humans to control or cover totally. In this respect it becomes necessary that "man" or "humankind" are not seen as separate realities from "nature" and "landscape" but rather as integral and recombinant parts of a continuum across the infinite. There is in all a consilience (see E. O. Wilson) that binds rather than slices the parts despite the scholarly effort to cut the whole into an increasing number of parts to give every PhD candidate or scholar a dissertation or essay theme. At some point we are led to assume

The situational ethics theory was advanced during the 1960's by Joseph Fletcher. It represents a middle ground position between antinomianism and legalism. Antinomianism (there is no law) posits that everything is relative to the moment and should be decided in a spontaneous fashion with man's will as the source of truth. Legalism follows a set of predetermined and different laws for every decision-making situation. Among situational ethicists are Emil Brunner, Reinhold Niebuhr, and John A.T. Robinson. For Fletcher the absolute law is love (*agape*) applied to all circumstances. A connection to this ethic can be found in the effort to idolize or formalize Nature.

"Since all things are caused or causers, assisted or assistants, mediated or mediators and all are linked by natural and invisible bonds that tie the more distant and the more different, I hold it impossible to know the parts without knowing the whole no more than to know the whole without knowing the parts in particular"
Blaise Pascal. **Pensées**. Article II. Garnier-Flammarion. Paris. 1976. Translation: German Cruz

"It is direction, not intention, that determines destination"
Andy Stanley. **The Principle of the Path**. Thomas Nelson. 2011

that the slice is the whole loaf and then we dice the slice into croutons with the same pretense until absurdity takes over. Pascal dealt with this issue in his development of calculus (integration and differentiation). It might behoove designers to study calculus as a philosophical tool for understanding as Pascal and Leibnitz intended rather than an esoteric mathematical conjuration (A magic spell or incantation/A magic trick or magical effect).

If design is a means to truth rather than a mere expression of limitations imposed or real, a search for spiritual congruency needs to be understood as a primary pilgrimage pathway. Without a doubt, the absence of a spiritual element in design weakens the outcome and takes away meaning and contextuality. The spiritual cannot be replaced with the intellectual or the morally neutral. Fear of religion is often argued as a reason for spirit adverse design outcomes, yet a love for mythology is endorsed as "spiritual" as much as filters are endorsed as proper screens for tobacco smoke. The issue is not religion (system) but rather faith (con-fidence is a faith synonym = with faith). The ability to engage and inquire without fear independent of a thought controlling system. Nature is not a spiritual substitute whether in Gaia love formulations or Earth preservation entelechies, regardless of heartfelt eagerness and intellectualized formulations. The pilgrim must face the truly spiritual that is BEYOND rather than the convenient substitute that lies under human control. The BEYOND is the goal rather than the conveniently NEAR. The pilgrim's path is in all truth a destination based on direction rather than intention (Andy Stanley). It is not a winsome and capricious tracing on invented ground. Sugar is bad for my health in any form and no amount of dialogue and protestation can change that fundamental fact. The sugar industries and well meaning nutritionists and food advocates will hector about particular programs and substitute products; however, the fundamental fact is that sugar is bad for me in any form and packaging. My health BEYOND is sugar free. That is true. There is no substitute.

Pilgrimage and Place

Certainly, form is not the entire scope of design action. It can be argued that is far from a dominant strategy or pathway. Place seems a more plausible pursuit. Landscape architecture has a well defined position (mission) in the design (creation) of places. This positional creative effort is imbued of extensive meaning and as such defines and focuses the design action and outcome more in *a posteriori* than *a priori* terms. The outcome is better known upon its completion rather than within its transit (pilgrimage) or its origen. In order to further understand its outcomes, the discipline would do well to engage more critically and creatively at all stages by study of the process and its anatomical structure (physiology) in consultation with other disciplines. Certainly, we perform much analysis and produce engaging charts of process that often have very little to do with outcome and serve more as justifications than reasons. The understanding and articulation of the autochthonous is habitually absent in favor of the indulgence of the personal. However, in landscape architecture there is no capacity for dominance of pure art in light of its space creating purpose. Phenomenologists like Edward Casey along with geographers like Yi-Fu Tuan and philosophers like Gaston Bachelard and Henri Lefebvre plus *enfants terribles* like Michel De Certeau, have explored the meaning of places and their ontological evolution and importance across history as well as in current times. Whether in abstract or in concrete form, place represents a position that form by itself cannot produce.

Casey wonders if the organic character of place and its ensuing capacity for growth places humans in the unique position to understand the human activity in places that will increase our awareness of inclusivity as a dominant quality that rescues us from past and current ignorance or indolence relative to place and its meaning to our existence and community. This view of place as an "incubator" of human activity places a burden for honesty in the design process where form is not the sole determinant component. This ultimate "limitless openess" of place (space) will enable plenitude or completeness that is BEYOND the capacity of form or could be the meaning giver to form. The exultant feeling of arriving at the end of a pilgrimage. The "eureka" moment of design labors. Of course, I am writing unbounded by protocols of philosophy and rhetorical structure in making vast connections in the manner of spiderweb building. The acrobatics of a spider in space might not

Edward Casey. **The Fate of Place**. California.1997

Yi-Fu Tuan. **Space and Place**. Minnesota.2001

Gaston Bachelard. **The Poetics of Space**. Beacon Press. 1994

Henri Lefebvre. **The Production of Place**. Wiley-Blackwell. 1992

Michel de Certeau. **The Practice of Everyday Life.** California. 1984

"Sometime during my study of the Dark Ages, I uncovered an odd paradox that exists in our minds about time gone by. It is a difference between history and the past. Simply stated, the past is what is real and true, while history is merely what someone recorded" Andy Andrews. **How Do You Kill 11 Million People.** Thomas Nelson. 2011

Single paths connect in a spiderweb system to form a universe flowing in the same direction

be far from the pilgrimage of designers, while the resulting web eventually makes sense by fitting in both the place and the wind driven jumps (of course, spiders have built in biological mechanisms for web making other than response to wind).

The pilgrimage thematic or ethos is dominant throughout ages and places. This is to say that after all is said and done the transforming outcome of the pilgrimage stands unchanged no matter the way or style of the march, and flows consequentially without force from the process itself. There is a responsive and responsible outcome well rooted in context that stands as the appropriate (Olmsted properly called it "fit") outcome. Thus, pretext surrenders to context upon digestion of all factors rather than vice-versa. Design outcomes flow naturally from a walking process rather than an intellectual or modal imposition. This might sound a bit too definitive and non-consensual for current tastes and trends in our late post-modern age; however, when we examine the work of designers across time and location (place), whether schooled or self-taught, we can discern a common response that can best be called a pilgrimage product free from any socio-religious dogma or rigidity. This final clarity is made possible by the pilgrimage walk where a reiterative recombinant (DNA) refining process removes the influence of non-essential elements. The arrival point of the pilgrimage then welcomes a cleaner and purer thought that becomes strong (compelling) by reason of its overcoming of testing and challenge over time and distance. This place of arrival is unique yet common. As physical designers we create places rather than situations. From Bachelard to Casey and Tuan and Lefebvre and Certeau, the search and evaluation of place has taken many routes yet arrived at a common location in person and perception. It is all about what we see and feel as individuals informed by context and truth. Of course, common perceptions arise by comparative agreement rather than enforced consensus. Both Maya Lin's Vietnam Memorial and Peter Walker World Trade Center/9-11 Memorial, elicit a commonality of perceptions (emotive and intellectual) and share a rather minimalist design response; but within each visitor, there is the uniquely personal that endures and responds with diversity. In this sense the pilgrimage has no real ending as it continues meaning in those who share it. The pilgrim is a conduit of the pilgrimmage experience to be shared with others before and after.

It all begins with a horizon line meeting a line traced from here to there with another line rising at the intersection(Euclid). A spider facing the abyss tosses a first web line across the infinite before a perspectival scheme. The horizon line defines a task to be done and a context for the doing. The vanishing line becomes a pathway or a pilgrimage route while the intersecting line provides connectivity up and down. It is upon this congruency that contact will be made with knowledge and will also come eventually to bring an understanding of the scale of the task. Standing at the point of origen, we face the challenge of getting to the horizon and then finding out what is the doing we are compelled to do. In all, the spiderweb testifies to a process upon the scheme. The journey is not immediate or free of obstacles. It might be short or long and often responds more to the spirit than to the flesh or the intellect. There might be examples and memories of other journeys but each journey is unique on its own accord. We just set out for the horizon with some tools and big expectations. The web will capture the space.

Thomas Seely has spent his life observing bees as much as Edward O. Wilson has studied the behavior of ants. From the life of these insects in the Hymenoptera (membrane winged) order, both scientists have developed a correlative understanding of human actions and habits that speak of a causal condition common in creation (or evolution, if you please). To Wilson this indicates consilience in and across the natural world much to the chagrin of those partial to a fractured universe. The hymenoptera order is characterized by its sociability that is expressed in regimented social systems with special order and assignments of conduct and labor.

Seeley sees in bees a very structured system of community building that involves site selection as well as community organization. This process he calls "swarm intelligence" shared with other species (locusts, fish, birds, termites, etc) and anchored by two principles: enthusiasm and flexibility from which four lessons can be taken:

> 1.- *Compose the decision-making group of individuals with shared interests and mutual respect*
> 2.- *Minimize the leader's influence on the group's thinking*
> 3.- *Seek diverse solutions to the problem*
> 4.- *Aggregate the group's knowledge through debate*

These lessons along with the principles, apply as much as to ordering a sandwich as to engage the planning and execution of a pilgrimage. Nobody walks alone as much as no idea is restricted

A single spiderweb represents a victory over fear and darkness. A feat of courage and skill rather than a celebration of whimsy.

Thomas Seely. **Honeybee Democracy.** Princeton. 2010
Edward O. Wilson. **On Human Nature**. Harvard. 1978/2004
_____. **Consilience: The Unity of Knowledge.** Vintage. 1999
_____. **The Ants.** Harvard, 1990

to a particular dimension. While a pilgrimage responds to very personal forces and concerns, it invariably relates to others equally engaged or peripheral to it, immediate or distant. For centuries, veritable human swarms have crossed Europe to reach Santiago de Compostela and Finisterre (end of the earth) seeking a high spiritual prize that became also a cultural legacy with lasting impact and everfresh insight. Human swarms not unlike bee swarms generate culture (society) and a place (beehive) for development of that culture. It is interesting to ponder how the bee settlements produced wax that was used to make the candles used to light the *scriptoria* (writing rooms) where history was recorded in the convents and abbeys where knowledge found refuge.

Getting BEYOND (Santiago) was exulting and marching 3 or 4 additional days (115 km) from Santiago to Finisterre and Muxia (on the far tip of the continent) represented a capstone. The ancients reached the shores of the Atlantic at a place called Punta de la Barca (Point of the Boat) with trepidation of having reached the end of the earth as far as they knew. This was the point where the land reached as far as possible into the darkness of the waters in the west. The point where the stone boat with the remains of the Apostle James hit the coast. But, it might also have been possible for some of them to wonder about the places that were hidden BEYOND the horizon just like Columbus observed from the piers at Palos de Moguer the sailmasts of ships emerging over the horizon to confirm the roundness of the Earth and the challenging promise of the unknown. Perhaps the portents of many years on the edge of the world are rightfully expressed by the words of the Beatnick poet Kenneth Patchen (1911-1972)3 when he writes:

> *The Impatient Explorer*
> *Invents a Box*
> *Where all Journeys*
> *May be Kept*

This might well be the task of the pilgrim upon consideration of the journey . . .

Walking as a Mental Attitude

The key element of a pilgrimage is the walking to be done between stages as well as between beginning and end. For many, the daily walk represents a confrontation with weather and topography while for others it is a matter of will and faith as well as endurance (physical/mental conditioning). There has to be will to do and faith (determination) to guide the going.

From Le Puy en Velay to Santiago de Compostela there are approximately 1,760,000 steps (assuming a flat land) which translates to about 7,040 steps per hour. Statistically it amounts to 266,666 steps per day in a 66 day journey. The numbers are often confusing by sheer dimension and might not be truly significant. Nobody can fairly assess the value and cost of every step taken by somebody else. From experience I found some days wonderful for walking and covering distance with grace and ease while on other days the feet simply refused to enjoy the exercise and the walk became a slogging activity with little joy. Yet, there is reason to rejoice in the outcome as well as in the transit. Getting there (beyond) was often more exciting than the departure (now). In this tone, Henry David Thoureau (1817-1862) was an ardent supporter of walks in nature doing about 4 hours every day and spoke on several ocassions of the benefits to body, mind, and soul (spirit) of a walking regime. Along with Thoreau, Americans have had a long tradition of escaping to Nature and rapsodizing about the woods and fields. Abraham Lincoln was a woodsman in his youth and Jens Jensen rendered homage to this with The Lincoln Memorial Garden (designed in 1935 and planted in 1936-39) on the south shore of Lake Springfield with acorns sent by school children. Today a large oak forest stands as a fitting memorial to the 16th president. Perhaps, Peter Walker had a corresponding idea with the 9-11 Memorial in New York. Before the successful design engagement with Central Park (1858), Frederick Law Olmsted (1822 - 1903) did in 1850 a rather extensive 1-month walking tour of England and Wales (*Walks and Talks of an American Farmer in England*) that had some traces of the Thoreau approach and established disciplinary and philosophical routes for the eventual development of landscape architecture . . .

Over time we have lost the desire to walk by reason of isolation, life/time demands, and automobilization. It is akin to social conditioning like animals in zoo cages or chicken coops in the farm. We become

---

"What is it that makes it so hard sometimes to determine whither we will walk? I believe that there is a subtle magnetism in Nature, which, if we unconsciously yield to it, will direct us aright. It is not indifferent to us which way we walk. There is a right way; but we are very liable from heedlessness and stupidity to take the wrong one. We would fain take that walk, never yet taken by us through this actual world, which is perfectly symbolical of the path which we love to travel in the interior and ideal world; and sometimes, no doubt, we find it difficult to choose our direction, because it does not yet exist distinctly in our idea".

"So we saunter toward the Holy Land; till one day the sun shall shine more brightly than ever he has done, shall perchance shine into our minds and hearts, and light up our whole lives with a great awakening light, so warm and serene and golden as on a bank-side in Autumn".

Henry David Thoreau. **On Walking.** Atlantic Monthly. 1862. (Lecture given at Concord Lyceum on April 23, 1851, published posthumously)

Frederick Law Olmsted. **Walks and Talks of an American Farmer in England.** U. Of Massachusetts. 2003

---

what the prison cell dictates. Oddly, we can travel faster and farther but we do not go far. Our attention is focused within a domesticated environment anchored in electronic and mechanical entertainment that pretend to give us pleasure and meaning *ex nihilo*. We walk long hours indoors in a treadmill to shape our bodies for display rather than endurance in a rather solitary pursuit of completeness. We consume special foods and read specialized simple books forsaking true reading (walking to know) that demands mental engagement rather than mere optical aerobics. We have become indiscriminate consumers of technology or viceversa while also becoming woefully ignorant of reality past and present. The outdoors are often substituted for a treadmill ride that emulates topography while Nature becomes just a television show, an easy read book or some convenient meme *or cause du jour* that tugs at our hearts and poses no challenge to our mind and spirit. Our most vexing problem has been widely diagnosed as obesity with a magic pill prescription solution except that our mind and our soul are also obese and slow moving, sluggish and pill adverse. Our real problem is indolence that can best be described as a degenerative disease of the spirit. The only solutions are spiritually based regenerative engagements alien to our culture and status. Of course, we drown in "spirituality" without spirit as advanced by a plethora of guides and gurus that offer man-made concoctions of spiritless essence that respond well to our fear of losing control or doing what we do not want to do. It is dangerous to rescue a drowning person lest you perish in the good effort. Yet, a drowning person is not a swimmer by simply being in the water. Thus, the pilgrimage has no power or effect without a key ingredient of the BEYOND which is under the authority of spirit. Somewhere in the time and distance dimension the spirtual void demands response that provides the critical direction for walking in Nature rather than a living room or an exercise hall. There is no substitute for truth. Sadly, we know this only in the empirical sense free from conviction.

On a contrary vein, Europeans greatly enjoy walking and have developed extensive networks for pedestrians and cyclists. Of course, we can argue that there is a vast difference between their dimension and ours. We are a larger country with robust needs and pleasures while Europe is a smaller continent with decidedly socialist structures of culture and governance that pose severe limits to individuality and independence (from our perspective). This might be true, except that our much vaunted freedom has been surrendered to a brainless slavery (slothfulness) to mechanics, pap discourses, and electronic games. The power of Nature to enrich our lives as suggested by Thoreau is disconnected from our lives in favor of inane substitutes that appeal to lowest common denominators and false concepts of importance and urgency. Walking from the front door to the car or from the parking lot to the office is not by any means a true walking experience as it is not a drive through a forest preserve or a national park. Our feverish support for "environmentalist causes" belies our indololence and promotes a false *status quo* that probably needs direction *(status quo vadis?* = where are you going?) rather than greater affirmation or false directions.

"Sport is a matter of technique and rules, of scores and competitions, needing apprenticeship, knowledge of positions, incorporation of proper style. And eventually, after all, improvisation and talent . . . to walk all you need is legs, nothing else . . . To walk is not a sport. Once erect, man had no choice but to walk"

Fréderic Gros. **Marcher, Une Philosophie**. Flammarion. 2011 (new edition).

Michel Jourdan, Jacques Vigne. **Marcher, Méditer**. Albin Michel. 1994/1998

Christophe Lamoure. **Petit Philosophie du Marcheur.** Editions Milan. 2007

Ian McHarg. **Design with Nature.** The Natural History Press. 1969

Donald Appleyard and Kevin Lynch. **The View from the Road**. MIT. 1965

Kevin Lynch. **Image of the City**. MIT/Harvard. 1960

Lewis Mumford. **The City in History**. Harcourt, Brace, and World. 1961

The Grande Randonnée system of long distance footpaths routed throughout France has well numbered routes akin to a major national highway system. Along with well designed walking routes and convenient access to refuges, gites and hostels complemented with supply outlets. There is a general philosophy or way of thinking developed around the walking action that engages the intellect both current and historic. People are able to walk for both pleasure and fitness as well as for knowledge of place. It is not just mere sport or hedonism. It is rather a finding of person and place. To this effect, Fréderic Gros (*Marcher, une philosphie*) offers a collection of excerpts from various writers and philosophers in support of a mental and spiritual justification rather than merely a sporting action. Gros blends Kerouac, Nietzsche, Rimbaud, Rousseau with Thoreau, Kant, Gandhi, and Holderlin into a powerful articulation of cultural and personal need for a walking regime. Gros wholeheartedly supports a clear ethical position integral to human life rather than a temporary effort after a fashion or a fad. The selection of authors is not restricted to age, time or position. Of course, there is the presumption that people would like to read and engage what is read with consequential impact upon life. In further development of the walking ethic, Michel Jourdan and Jacques Vigne (*Marcher, méditer*) examine the inner motivation for walking as a conduit for meditation. A way to recapture lost thought and recover consciousness of self and place. On the same philosphical route (march? pilgrimage?) Christophe Lamoure (*Petit Philosphie du Marcheur*) addresses walking as a personal quest both moral and intellectual concurrent with all of life. Thus, walking is integrated as a physical and philosophical act. The physical engages the body while the mental (philosophical) engages mind and spirit. It demands thinking about self as much as about the land, the climate, the entire context of environment. The total dimension of being is then captured in the simple action of walking.

Thus, walking conveys a mental attitude that engages not only the physical exercise aspects but also the intellectual and the spiritual. It is not merely a thought or a fancy but rather a full body engagement. One walks with the mind rather than solely with the feet since the body is a total tri-dimensional unity. The advance across land promotes a progressive change of perspective that enlarges the understanding (perception) to the benefit of knowledge acquisition and development. Lamoure's view of completeness in the walking experience is aptly illustrated by the effort in design practice to produce statistically supported data comparative sets of land and culture features that were started with the use of hand technology overlays (Ian McHarg, *Design with Nature)* and soon advanced to sophisticated digital computer overlay processes (GIS/CAD) as a means to understanding the inherent and comparative attributes of the landscape (including urban areas). The work with "Nature" proposed by McHarg links quite effectively with the advocacy of "Balance with Nature" by Lewis Mumford (*The City In History)* to suggest a more direct and comprehensive engagement than a mere arms-length clinical and one-dimensional approach. Somehow, a new way of thinking has emerged that promotes a measure of walking contact with the land as a means to understand and to know as a pre-condition to effective design intervention. Roughly contemporary to the advocacy of Mumford and the technical advances of McHarg, urban and human geographers (Urban Morphologists) like M. R. G. Conzen (1907 - 2000) at the University of Newcastle upon Tyne and his son Michael P. Conzen (University of Chicago) employed a methodology ("Town-Plan Analysis") that is generally related to GIS and CAD and applicable to the historical study of urban form. This bridging of disciplines translates into clarity (truth) of mutual benefit.

Therefore, the issue of attitude relates to a disciplinary approach rather than a mere single posture. The current work of leading landscape architects makes extensive use of GIS and graphic digital technology to analyze and represent both real conditions and proposed outcomes that inform more completely about the site and its context/content. The availability of land data and accesible technology make sophisticated site analysis and design presentation possible in real terms. The problem is now an excess of "reality" that makes the process products unreachable by human perceptive capacities. There is only so mucu "perfection" humans can understand and access. With the addition of "humane touches" (hand drawing, hand coloring, hand lettering) these representations are made more humane (empathic) and promote a better understanding (knowledge) of outcomes that are not emotionally based but rather intellectually (rationally) rooted. This is not to say that emotion is not a component of design decisions or outcomes. All of design expresses emotion as it comes from human engagement and imagination; however, it is justified by a rational argument that addresses needs and expectations beyond the very private concerns of the designer since the gioal is to "design for others" rather than fulfill personal desires and notions.

Attribution is a serious issue of concern although it often distracts from purpose. Students have a very difficult time with the omission of I-me-mine in presentations of their work. This absence of universality is seen clearly in their work as well as in that of more mature designers ever attentive to attribution and ownership. Very much like Michelangelo carving his name (MICHELANGELUM) on the sash across Mary's chest in the *Pietá* at St. Peter's Basilica. There is a human need for attribution and retribution upon execution of well thought out work or even minimally competent expressions. Design outcomes exist in a realm above common use (the designer's mind) yet must relate to common users. It is a quandary that designers must confront with skill rather than verbal expressions of regret. The focus for the designer must be set primarily in the directional clarity (truth) of the path rather than merely upon the acceptance of a fashionable outcome. As Andre Gide (1869 - 1951) puts it: *"let the importance be placed upon how you see rather than upon in the object of your sight"* (*Les Nourritures Terrestres*). Esentially, the value of work rests beyond its approval if executed with integrity. It is not a sign of humility to remain silent in expectation of praise but it is true that only the author has a notion as to the value of work. Any value given beyond the author is an assignation that errs above or below the true value (even when made by peers). When properly executed, the work of a designer appears simple and easy by reason of the synthetic transit between NOW and NEAR. This is true even in design education. Any monkey can swing from trees high in the canopy except that not everybody is a monkey. A high measurte of respect must be given to the monkeys unless one has the skill to do what they do. Silent attribution dressed in respect (remuneration) is a high form of compliment. We should expect not less and use that

André Gide. **Les Nourritures Terrestres.** Gallimard. 1942

point for further education. In this lies the formation of attitude as an expression of life through capacity and capability.

The walk experience is important as a means of learning as much as a framing of competence. It informs the designer and the client about process and atttributes. Thanks to current advances, the physical walking of land and site can be undertaken to a certain extent by technologically based steps with the understanding that

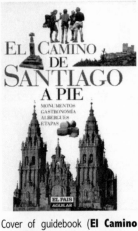

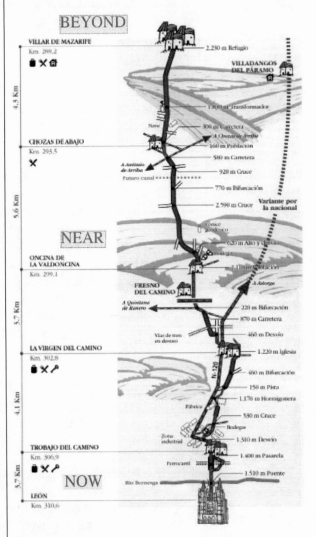

Cover of guidebook (**El Camino de Santiago a Pie/The Road of Santiago on Foot**) expresses the concept of NOW - NEAR - BEYOND while the same effect is accomplished with a map for a journey. The pilgrim can see the evolving sense of order to the journey in tune with localities, landmarks, intersections, and arrival points. The journey is revealed one step at a time. The information level is not minute but sufficient to execute the walk or seek additional information from other sources. The tone and style of the graphics serves to set a tone also that speaks of walking methodically rather than moving fast across the land.

some particularities need a personal presence for proper appreciation. During the walk on the Camino; despite extensive background on the land and its topography, it was not possible to understand its magnitude and impact until feet were planted on real ground and eyes as well as muscles could connect and speak to mind. This analogy can apply to the connection between eye/hand/pencil in the classic notion of perception or eye/mouse/screen in its current version. Both require a going out to site in order to fully comprehend magnitude and qualities. In the abstract, the daily journeys of the marches on the Camino were easy to comprehend in terms of distance, time and attributes (see map in page 18); however, slope and ground character dictated a daily particularity that while generally similar was unique. The 16 km between Le Puy and Montbonnet were totally different in tonality and rigor than the 14.5 km between Montbonnet and Monistrol d'Allier as much as the roughly equal 28 km marches between Leon and Villadangos del Páramo and Villadangos and Astorga appeared to have been. In the absence of a common dominant element, the attitude (habit of doing) needs to be constant. It drives as well as delimits approach and engagement. Getting there is not merely a question of covering distance but rather of containing the sensual experience of distance in the mind. It is the attitude (habit) built upon knowledge and awareness (educated perception) that serves as both guide and motivator.

NOW

NEAR

BEYOND

OUTER BEYOND
(Legacy / Patrimony)

The Design Pilgrimage Path as a
Walk toward clarity and definition.

Steps to Seeing

The major purpose of the design pilgrimage is the development of a competent capacity to see with clarity enlarged by reasonable inquiry. This implies a journey of careful investigation and evaluation of facts (Truths) with full engagement of reason rather than emotion. By reasons of cultural and political focus the action of seeing is often clouded with screened and presumptive images that hide the true subject and object. Many false images and options rise to demand attention and struggle for dominance under various attractive but dangerous appeals. These appeals to falsehood are very much like the siren songs in the Odyssey that almost drove Ulysses and his sailors insane. The need to see truthfully and clearly is not widely accepted nowadays since it entails a commitment to a clearly correct path independent of distraction and presumptiveness. Walking on this true path promotes a unity of purpose between subject and object that enables greater understanding and consequent knowledge. With seeing in truth rather than merely looking there is a knowledge outcome that is transcendent rather than superficial or innocuous. This capacity to enhance seeing is tri-dimensional (mind/body/spirit) and demands surrendering of pre-conceptions and blinders or screens. As with birth, this surrender is a naked (divested) action. It is done in truth with sensitivity to virtues of goodness (utility) and beauty (presence). Love enters in the doing but it is not a pretext to action. Thus, it has not a situational ethos or segmented interest. It is total (integral) at all times. Since design happens in life and viceversa, it is applicable to both equally and concurrently. Somehow it is outside the formal law (strictures of design)and supports individual expression in both execution and outcome. This outline represents a basic structure that has no formal configuration yet formulates a process or schema.

1. A Change in Perception

It is critical for the pilgrim to have a real or intended change in the manner of seeing. It is not just an ocular issue but one that engages the entire body and mind. From barely glimpsing (to know imperfectly, to conjecture by indications) to looking (superficial awareness) to seeing (deep understanding) there is progression of knowledge that cannot be shortcut or equivocated. From afar the place in the NEAR must be embraced with all senses in an unleashing of appetite (unstoppable hunger) and sensuality (total use of the senses) as well as thought and essence. It is not a matter of physical sex but rather of total immersion (tri-dimensionally) in a task in pursuit of a positive outcome.

From Far to Near and Beyond

As the spider on the edge prepares to jump into the weaving of a web, perception begins in the NOW with a view that seeks orderly clarity in the middle field (NEAR) along with supported or informed clarity to reach BEYOND. The spider looks for a landing spot rather than any place. There is a plan in mind that needs contextualization in execution. Clarity is the purpose (direction) even in the darkness. The objective is always focused in the NEAR. From the NOW to the NEAR there is a transaction of all manner and quantity of data that is refined in a pilgrimage process to the middle (the NEAR) and critically analyzed further to provide a basis for action that can take us BEYOND. The solution is then pure and clear. It fits well the problem and the context, as well as, the capacity and capability of the designer. In this manner, clear solutions endure by force of their compelling simplicity (Lincoln Memorial in Springield, Illinois by Jens Jensen) while others obscure the clarity with an overwhelming amount of subtext and emotion (Memorial to the Mudered Jews of Europe in Berlin, Germany by Peter Eisenman and Bruno Happold). It is not saying that one is better or more worthy than the other. What is important is the simple eloquence of one versus the contrived elegance of the other. It is simply a case of metaphorical clarity as when we say: *the sky is blue* rather than give a list of tonalities and similitudes that obscure the first image. A radical and still simple statement would also be the poetic line from Paul Eluard: *"The sky is blue like an orange"* that surprises by contrast.

It is also quite possible that arrival at the NEAR will uncover a need for additional data that can provide greater clarity as well as reiterative returning steps toward the NOW (point of beginning) necessary to add value and meaning to the clarity. It is all akin to travel through a microscope with lens adjustments back and forth. In the first step atop the NOW there is a compelling issue of chance. Design is not a prescription for exact travel as much as path in an open field toward a desirable end. A chance taken courageously in the expectation of greater gain. Gilles Deleuze (1925-1995) did extensive work on historical philosophers and engaged Nietzche in a study of the idea of a chance game of dice in *Thus Spake Zarathustra* as a roll between earth and sky. Night and day struggle with each other while the moments of throwing and rolling become

"The current difficulty in clarity of the concept of landscape is not without a connection to a progressive and truly illusory liberation from the territorial context. The earth is not anymore the sole provider for our needs and we have brought to the scene signs and images that do not fit the consistency of the world. The reality of the senses is erased behind curtains of our own creation. Sciences, and particularly those of the landscape, have largely contributed to this dysfunctionality; they have built screens before reality to build isolated areas of interest; they have broken relationships, disarticulated mountains, they have dried up the source of all signs of landscape, those that shoot between the phenomena, in the intervals where flows and correspondences are established".

Michel Corajoud. **Preamble/The Landscape is the Place Where the Sky and the Earth Touch** (Le Paysage c'est l'endroit ou le Ciel et la Terre se Touchent) Actes Sud/ENSP. Versailles.2010 Translation: Germán Cruz

Gilles Deleuze. **The Dice Throw**. In Margaret Iversen (ed). **Documents of Contemporary Art.** MIT Press. 2010.

"The mind being prepared beforehand with the principles most likely for the purpose . . . incubates in patient thought over the problem, trying and rejecting, until at last the proper elements come together in the view, and fall into their places in fitting combination"

Alexander Bain. **The Senses and the Intellect.** University Publications of America. Washington D.C. 1855/1977. Cited by R Keith Sawyer. **Explaining Creativity: The Science of Human Innovation.** Oxford. 2006 (p67)

the same. Each dice reproduces itelf endlessly until the proper combination is reached. *"The dice throw affirms becoming and it affirms the being of becoming"* (The Dice Throw) in the same way that the spider begins its web jumping by chance into the infinite. In weaving, the spider is being and becoming concurrently along with the web. The spider reaches out not so much to find a final point but merely to establish another landing to hold the web. It is a daring effort. Web weaving is not an arm's length activity or a distanced viewing by electronic means and video connection. Spider and web need to touch each other all throughout the effort. It is a sensual recombinant process where each becomes in the other. In all, each becomes clearer by repetition. There are few one line webs attached to a single side. The arrival at the train station in Le Puy en Velay was a spider jump moment where the walk (like the first strand of a web) was affixed to an edge at the feet of a mountain range with our stage destinations still hidden in the horizon behind fog and vegetation as well as the slopes of successive mountain ranges. Yet, we knew of the route, we had plans, as well as reservations in secure landings. The web still needed to become.

From Seeing to Understanding

Once something is truly and clearly seen (free of filters), the mind can be unleashed to understanding rather than mere acknowledgement of knowledge. Walking through the woods in Gascogne or Galicia, there was no sight of town or steeples but the road was marked by a pictogram painted at different places and had to be trusted to be correctly placed (intended) to take us to the desired destination. Many times it was hard to see the signs on first instance and they were found in the most unexpected places. The signs were two simple bands of color (red/white) or a sea shell (coquille) or a yellow arrow painted on trees, walls, pavement, or stones. As one got used to reading (understanding) the road, the signs became easier to see and find. We had assurance of being on the right road by the experience from hundreds of years and thousands of pilgrims who had made the same journey before plus maps and guides and a fresh developed intuitive sense of wayfinding. Intuition being considered as a developed (acquired) form of knowledge rather than an expontaneous manifestation of deeply held unaware knowledge. In the open country the path was often clear but in villages and cities the markings often succumbed to construction or the vagaries of urbanity. Nevertheless, at the right time we arrived to our destinations and celebrated the certainty as well as the route and the finding. We knew from previous learning and current experience that the path was there (it had been there for centuries before) although we had not experienced it directly. This knowledge kept us on track and made us realize when and if we strayed away. In some measure we became one with the path and viceversa. So is with the design journey.

Achieving knowledge is different from knowledge utilization. All the information we had acquired enabled the journey and the completion of stages in the journey enriched our understanding that was then stored as practical knowledge. Whether as a spider or a honey bee or an ant, the pilgrim or designer carves out a route based on chance, swarming, or territorial search supplemented by the knowlege transmitted from previous generations (DNA). Each approach engaged context, resources, and needs while seeking clarity (understanding) of direction as well as success of arrival. A negative answer in a calculus equation indicates the need to balance that will produce a positive result. Integration and differentiation will work toward completeness rather than inconclusiveness. Being and becoming complement each other. So it is with design, understanding the contextual evaluation of structures and components by themselves as well as together represents a platform upon which further action can be pursued in all assurance of transiting upon a correct path. It can take the form of layers or sections or illustrative charts as much as it can also be an educated response by previous practice or intuition.

The intuitive response is something akin to muscle memory that enables quick thinking with minimal error. The memorized multiplication tables of our childhood remain operative across life. Even patients with various degrees of memory loss are able to remember a few or all the tables as normal events in their lives. While psychology looks at intuition as the acquisition of knowledge without the benefit of reason, it might be good to look at it as a conditioning of reason with knowledge to shorcut elaborate thinking processes by the rather automatic use of previously acquired knowledge. A direct awareness of truth. As mentioned above, the traditional mathematical drills during elementary school by which addition and multiplication tables were memorized represent an early form of intuition building. The process is replicated in some aspects of language acquisition under a rote system (a fixed, habitual, or mechanical course of procedure) or apparent automatic actions of daily life like closing garage doors, making coffee, turning off

Fredom is not the absence of core. It is really the affirmation of a core that sustains and supports.

Serendip relates to an ancient name for Sri Lanka and a story published in 1557 by Michele Tramezzino in Venice. It purports to be a Persian fairy tale relating the adventures of three princes who by "accident and sagacity" solve the nature of a lost camel. From here "serendipity" has been assigned to events that produce a positive outcome free from rigor.

some lights or reading favorite sections of the daily newspaper. Knowledge becomes in being. The answers are immediate and trustworthy because they are built confidently in memory with no need of further proofing. In explanations of creativity by cognitive psychology, this intuition is referred to as insight that presupposes a deep seeing rather than a mere looking (Alexander Bain and others). This "mind eye" sits at the center of significant perception in design. Not just "looking" but "seeing" with intensity of meaning (semiotics/semiology).

The old master-apprentice system promoted the transfer of knowledge by mentorship and tradition while we now enable the apprentices to run on their own like children flying in wind drifts away from Charlotte's web apparently free from heritage except for the DNA still imbeded in their systems. This fracturization of the learning or acquisition of knowledge process appears on the surface to be eminently democratic and liberating; however, it contains vast elements of falsehood or imperfect knowledge that can lead to significant error or empty areas of awareness that are filled by suppositions without foundation. The master-apprentice system resolved this by practice interaction whereby the apprentice received guidance and instruction on practical fundamentals from which a personal expression (style) could be developed. Michelangelo learned from Domenico Ghirlandaio and passed in turn a developed form of knowledge to several apprentices who did mediocre work in art but wrote biographies that provided insight into the method of the master for other generations. Same thing with Leonardo and Raphael among the masters of the High Rennaisance. Our current system confers advanced degrees to candidates with little previous knowledge that are encouraged to explore the edges of the discipline and find "new knowledge" that in dissertation form enables the granting of advanced credentials for a teaching career bereft of practice. Most certainly, there is nothing wrong with exploring the boundaries; however, it is advisable to also know the material within boundaries as a proper context for what is bound. Knowing the skin of a helium balloon without knowing the gas within provides no foundational understanding of the lift that sustains the balloon although it might lead to a deep and emotional awareness of the properties of rubber. In a discipline as wide as landscape architecture, the knowledge of boundaries might lead to an awareness of mere city states within a large realm rather than knowledge and understanding of the realm. In walking through a historic pathway in France and Spain, the historical context is ever

Alexander Bain (1818-1903) Empiricist philosopher and educationalist from Scotland who advanced innovative concepts in psychology, linguistics, logic, moral philosophy and education reform. Founder of *Mind,* the first ever journal of psychology and analytical philosophy. Leading figure in application of the scientific method to psychology. Several of his works have been republished from old editions dating before 1923:

Mind and Body: The Theories and Their Relation. Nabu Press. 2010
Moral Science: A Compendium of Ethics. Nabu Press. 2010
Practical Essays. Qontro Classical Books. 2010

present and often overwhelmingly. Periods along history appear to blend into a mass of stone hard to understand without a map or diagram of its historical place. A Templar fortress emerges in the plain (Domaine du Sauvage) while a larger castle rises in a riverbank in a city (Ponferrada) to connect a sphere of protection from the 13th century across two countries and 500 miles. The Templar Knights were the "highway patrol" of the Middle Ages for pilgrims and travelers. This ancient presence of assistance and protection is contrasted with mounted Guardia Civil exercising the same role in our times. The limits (boundaries) seem to evanesce across time to give a larger context to the pilgrimage and the territory. Thus, the question is: where are the real boundaries and how do you know their dimension?

It might be argued in some circles that knowledge acquisition needs to obey certain rules and undergo a selected series of review processes by duly credentialed overseers in order for all pursuers to achieve an equal or comparable acceptable outcome. Kind of an enforcing body that ensures equal outcomes in traffic and approach. Clearly, this is not supported by natural or historical evidence and represents no more than an intellectual position or accommodation by a dominant group to a fashion or current deeply rooted in a presumed cultural niche or theory. It is doubtful that Galileo submitted his findings to a scientific set of peers before publication or that Einstein submitted to a filtration system of review and approval. So goes also for Pascal, Sartre, Tolstoi, Marx, Kafka, Nabokov, Hawking, Darwin, and others. They all took a risk and then welcomed critical input after publication rather than seek previous approval. Thus, design is informed by precedent but seeks no approval for performance. The notion that design inquiry needs guardrails as preventors of either faulure or heresy is rather new and seems to emerge from weakness in identity or knowledge of self as a professional and a role of significance within the discipline. Of course, this might be seen as an offensive statement by those who seek offense at all cost and in all places. Honestly, no offense is intended. The issue is one of control and assurance of safety that is alien to the design action. Michelangelo's work on the ceiling of the Sistine Chapel was born of an appreciation for talent demonstrated in other work, a confidence on skills refined over time, and a taking of risk yet to be demonstrated. The spider jumps and the pilgrim walks into an undefined NEAR trusting inquiry in truth to lead to a clear BEYOND. Most certainly, all BEYONDS are not equal or

Simon Bell, Ingrid Sarlöv Herlin, Richard Stiles. **Exploring the Boundaries of Landscape Architecture.** Routledge. 2012

identical. The convergent nature of inquiry need not lead to just one place or point. Such is freedom. Such is design.

While design is affected by fashion (rule of conduct or procedure/ custom), it cannot be enslaved to fashion dictates that deny its freedom and truth seeking mission. If I set out to travel cross-country from Chicago to San Francisco and end up in Sarasota, Florida, the purpose of the trip has been denied by false information or mistaken acquisition of knowledge. There might be consolation in the event of doing the traveling itself and the arrival to a destination, but it was not the intended purpose no matter how the argument may be constructed or construed. Both the NEAR and the BEYOND lacked clarity (truth) and the traveler lacked knowledge (NOW) or intuition sufficient to accomplish the task. There might not be intuitive knowledge in this traveling mode but it can be argued by some that there is a degree of innovation or a new way of doing and seeing. As such, innovation becomes the new catchword (*mot de jour*) for intuition because it does not require a knowledge acquisition effort. Thus, everybody can be creative for any reason at any time. Everybody can be a designer, Everybody can be innovative. All that remains is to assign special innovation boundaries to genders and races to compose a truly diverse and correct picture. Order is sacrificed to the benefit of lower expectations upon the finding of difficult portions in the path of truth. Alternative pleasant routings away from the main road.

The removal of order (clarity) has enabled so-called fresh expressions of "creative thinking" (Stanford Design Institute and others) to emerge and satisfy primarily the hunger for marketing commodities by swarms of fast climbing corporate executives and marketing directors. The familiar and the mundane are played as matters of the gravest importance for civilization. It is essentially a replication of the long played game of new model introductions in the automobile industry expanded across all industries. New model names, new gadgets on the dashboard, fresh seating covers, satellite connections for music and telephone, exciting color palettes and luxurious display of chrome parts all mounted on the same frame with generally the same internal combustion engine that Henry Ford rolled out the asembly line almost a century ago. Originality becomes mere re-packaging and creativity becomes innovation within the boundaries of spreadsheets and marketing hype. Thus, design becomes an accessible lowest common denominator lost in computer games and business school models. Whether design can

The third eye (also known as the inner eye) is a mystical and esoteric concept referring in part to the ajna (brow) chakra in certain Eastern spiritual traditions like Hinduism. Other religious faiths have adopted or identified this concept as a gate that leads to higher conciousness and a deeper inner experience. The third eye is often associated with visions, clairvoyance, precognition, and out-of-body experiences. Meditation schools and arts, such as yoga, many Chinese martial arts, Zen, and Japanese martial arts such as Karate and Aikido make extensive efforts to develop this third eye as a gate to higher consciousness.

In terms of Kabbalah, the Ajna chakra is attributed to the sphere of Chokmah or Wisdom. Others regard the third eye as corresponding to the non-emanated sephirah of da'ath (knowledge). From here, the concept bridges over to western traditions where it connects to its Eastern currents.

In the 19th century, Helena Blavatsky (1831-1891) founded the Theosophical Society and led a spiritualist discovery and awareness movement that advocated 7 basic constituent bodies (Physical/Ethereal/Vital/Animal Soul/Human Soul/Spiritual Soul/Spirit of Self). Her views and publications became in general terms the foundation of subsequent spiritualist movements and eventually fertilized the New Age. Although her theories are very much disputed nowadays, a remnant is still evident in our contemporary discourse of spirituality.

be considered a commodity is a discussion that is no longer worth having in the corporate world but still has currency in academia. For reasons of their own, academics live a few years removed from real time. More so at these times of reduced academic budgets, increased performance, utility (value) demands and heavy pressure for credentialing and digital measuring. Academically, on the edge of the NOW as well as in the center of the NEAR, the innovation emphasis or fad has produced vast masses of people surprised at outcomes they do not understand along with extrapolated imitations of "creative thinking" or "innovation" programs and procedures increasingly removed from their original direction. The pretense to ownership of terms and definitions feeds the arrogance of a few and the snobbery of many. With the addition of "Design" to any number of extinct academic degrees, the academy seeks reinvigoration and customer satisfaction. However, the market (the grand commercial stage) is volube and the product offerings share in the volubility with venal enthusiasm among the target populations. Somehow, academia has existed away from such realities but it is now forced to engage them under truly frightening circumstances. A new way of seeing is necessary or at least a refocusing and cleansing of the lenses. Getting to BEYOND might not matter anymore. Surviving in NOW has become the urgent thing to do. The mind falters without direction. Reality is as confusing as walking on a slippery Moebius strip.

Of course, there are now multiple views (interpretations) on "innovation" and the celebration of the "new" has taken over the stage whether in packaging old products in new skins or pursuing fresher ways to package corporate culture. In their March 2012 issue, *Fast Company* lists the "World's 50 Most Inovative Companies" with a definitive bias toward economic or technological success and dominance as the standard. Absent from consideration is the humane cultural impact as well as the long term utility of the company's endeavors. It is all well centered on market share, dominance, profitability, and advantageous use of technology. Innovation in this context is a property (commodity) of business schools focused upon "newness" of products and aggresive or agile strategies that produce substantial and fast returns. In this context, academia has a hard decision to make. Whether to be the web maker or the fly captured in the web. There is no middle way. Spiders do not enter into agreements of peaceful coexistence with their prey. The time of tweed jackets with elbow patches has passed. The world is new.

The saying: *"If at first you succeed, conceal your astonishment"* relates somewhat to unexpected outcomes (serendipity) and refers clearly to the creative product that is not expected. A fortunate outcome that is not understood except as an accident beyond rational processes. Thus, the design path is more properly defined as a search for truth based on the critical observation of internal and external relationships relevant to the assignment rather than an inductive effort to achieve a foreseen outcome. From the deductive method in design as well as other disciplines emerges knowledge rather than serendipity. The rigor of research and analysis demand it and produce it. In the second day of our walk in France after trudging down the steep stone face of a mountain with 30 lbs bagpacks pushing us down, we were happy to find at our hostel a service that would transport our bagpacks from station to station and free us from the burden to enable a better and more pleasant walk. It was a wonderful service that other pilgrims had also discovered. Eventually, we found out that the intricate effort to pick up and deliver bagpacks in many hostels and refuges scattered in hills and valleys demanded a great (intimate) knowledge of the region and the places as well as timing across distance in order to meet delivery and pick-up schedules. Not all walkers covered the same distance every day or started the daily journey at the same time and place. Moving like spiders weaving a large daily web, the couriers met their assignments with considerable accuracy and gentility. It was rather comforting to arrive at a destination and find bagpacks waiting. These couriers became very useful to us not only for transportation of bags but also for information about places and routes as well as relays for making reservations further down the road. Their innate knowledge (intution) served well to guide us and others to clarity. Moreover, as we moved from region to region, they connected to other similar services in the manner of linking webs across territories and places. Practical intuition had taken the road walking experience across centuries and done an apt translation for the 21st century. After the initial success, the carrier system found imitators eager to share on the benefits of a new business but ignorant of the knowledge necessary to conduct it successfully. After a season or two, these imitators ceased to be competitors. It is not that only one person can have the knowledge, but that there is a price to pay for knowledge acquisition with honest engagement of the route and the context, rather than merely wishing to do or expecting to receive it gratis (free of knowledge acquisition effort). The ruggedness of the mountains and the route produced equally rugged individuals strongly focused on mission rather than

For over 20 years, Rick Strassman MD, Clinical Associate Professor of Psychiatry at the University of New Mexico School of Medicine, has done research with psychedelic drugs involving the powerful naturally-occurring compound, DMT—N,N-dimethyltryptamine (**DMT: The Spirit Molecule.** 1999). He was led to the use of DMT through his earlier study of the partially dormant pineal gland that resides between the two hemispheres of the brain as a potential biological locus for spiritual experiences. In **Inner Paths to Outer Space** (2008), he has looked more carefully at the common "other worlds" experience that volunteers frequently reported during his research.

It is noted that various types of lower vertebrates, such as reptiles and amphibians, can actually sense light via a third parietal eye—a structure associated with the pineal gland—which serves to regulate their circadian rhythms, and for navigation, as it can sense the polarization of light.

wishful interlopers seeking a fashionable dividend or convenient entertainment. Such is also the nature of the pilgrimage walk.

2.- A Change in Reception

The journey from NOW to NEAR and BEYOND causes a progressive development of sensitivity (touching with mind and body) that increases (elongates) the meaning and extent (dimension) of the design action. The progress of inquiry demands a change in reception mode. It is no longer useful to merely sense but it is necessary to reach deeper (feel) with every sense (each sense contains extensions of the others). In *De Anima,* Aristotle declares the existence of only five senses and suggests that they are complementary to one another in the shaping of reality. Whatever our opinion of Aristotle, this fact remains unchanged. Thus, sensing deeply and knowingly is critical to the completion of any sensuality driven action. The problem is the use of one sense as dominant to the exclusion or development of the others unless we are forced by circumstances or accident. It is then rather easy to appreciate levels (intensities) of sensuality (use of senses) that augment the acqusition and utilization of knowledge.

Without engaging in a study of Eastern philosophical practices and particularly of martial arts, it is rather interesting to note how the pursuit of meditation disciplines leads to the development of an "inner eye" or its equivalent that augments the development of greater and deeper vision and awareness. Somehow, the pilgrim (designer)) needs to pursue this sensitivity for the sake of acquiring direction toward knowledge and clarity. It is not so much a mental exercise but a sensual attuning (make receptive or aware). Of course, we can say and assume that design is an activity independent of any spiritual or mental condition or discipline. Yet, in the same dialogue we might speak of inspiration. Of some stimulus that guides and gives meaning. From where does it come? How do we acquire it? Very much like a potter relating to clay, the extensive molding and re-molding action with the hand also involves the mind and the senses in an effort to give life to the lump and grant it a transformational power. A lump becomes an object. An object speaks of a motive. It might seem that we are touched as much as we also touch, that we are seen as much as we also see, etc.

The path from NOW to NEAR represents a challenge to the senses that requires us to engage (march) in a different way. It is not a simple matter of going from Point A to Point B. All along the path, expressions of touch by all senses actively pursue clarity through analysis and experience of influence factors no different than the accommodations of the spider to the various anchoring places. The spider web fits the context and contains all that is expected of it to do for the benefit of the spider. While for other observers the web is a wonderful figure with great evocative power, for the spider it is fundamentally a trap for food rather than an artistic expression or a means to pass away idle time. Conversely, landscape design has a focus in the creation of spaces for people rather than primarily in the representation of ideologies of beauty and communitiy or the showcasing of art and science. Those things are incidental rather than fundamental.That landscape can be used to mean things other than land and trees and textures is obvious since by design it is linked to human experience and history. Yet the knowledge acquisition still needs to be centered upon truth with additional connotations arising from the process rather than being assigned *ex post facto* (retroactively). It is all quite simple. Or is it?

Distant Touching

From afar, the stars are just bright sparks in the infinite. We watch them with awe and play at connecting dots to extract images that will trigger memory and recollection. Meaning moves from a mere distant light to a pictogram that denotes a concept or an ideation of meaning (semiotics). In assigning meaning we are touching the far object and bringing it to the NEAR. Across the galaxy, this touching of one star causes the touching of other bodies to provide context. Constellations emerge and the myths created in a few rocky isles in the Ionian and Aegean seas become enlarged and justified to inhabit not only zodiacs but literature and culture. Yet, the Greeks are not alone. New pilgrims come to share the road and strive to change the basics for confrontation under diverse guises. In their zeal for change the road cannot remain the same and needs to be appropriated and redefined for the sake of personal expression and identity pursuit. Thus, the vast infinite that contains us all becomes a personal infinite that contains only our self defined individuality. In this guise, each designer (pilgrim) is compelled to state unequivocally the content and extent of a new order separate from other orders before and after. For example, the traditional name of a discipline like landscape architecture with all its denotations and connotations might need to be abandoned in favor of a redefined dominion under a name like "landscape urbanism" or critically "reformulated" in a manifesto that purports to contain all that is new and worthwhile in a highly sophisticated world now seen by very special people in a manner obscured to all before them. Regardless of the legacy, there is now a fresher legacy with urgent needs seeking to overthrow the old without fully understanding the substance of the legacy itself. In identical manner, not unlike Cronus (who ate his children to prevent them from overthrowing him) practitioners in a revolutionary mode adopt what might represent a radically new view of certain select principles to provide new attributes to their work. Thus, we can speak of new biological processes as if there has been a new creation (or evolution) of biological beings and systems. The new redefined processes adapt desired features of others and introduce expressions of contrary or similar meaning. Yet, it is after all a new version of the old with convenient new vocabulary that eventually achieves the same outcomes but serves well to establish fame and build fortune or power bases. Upon close examination we are apt to discover that these new webs follow the path of other previous webs. The earth has been round for quite some time and people have been people for some of that time with periodic costume changes. Distance touching keeps us connected rather than isolated in our rebellions. We are able to see the full dimension of things rather than a narrow optical illusion. Constellations work together for the good of the cosmos rather than the satisfaction of a single star.

Immediate Touching

The MIT mathematician and meteorologist Edward Lorenz (1917 - 2008) was a pioneer in chaos theory and delivered a paper in 1963 on *"The Law of Sensitive Dependence Upon Initial Conditions"* to the New York Academy of Sciences. In essence the paper forwarded the hypothesis that *"a butterfly could flap its wings and set molecules of air in motion, whIch would move other molecules of air, in turn moving more molecules of air — eventually capable of starting a hurricane on the other side of the planet"*. Eventually, the presentation was augmented and entitled "The Butterfly Effect" (1972) at the 139th meeting of the American Association for the Advancement of Science under the more enticing title *"Predictability: Does the Flap of a Butterfly's Wings in Brazil Set off a Tornado in Texas?"*. The general idea is one of sequential connectivity caused by a small change in the initial condition of a system. The chain of events traceable to its most minute source shows a causality that is worth noting even at the larger scale. In design the "butterfly effect" relates well to the journey on the path between NOW, NEAR and BEYOND and could be re-stated as the impact of a single pencil point on a sheet of vellum. In the culture, the "butterfly effect" has been used extensively in wellness counseling (Dannielle Miller), marketing strategic plans, theological argumentation (Andy Andrews), gender choice impacts (Susan Hawthorn), political observations (James Swallow) and a wide assortment of loosely related discussions that seek to prove on particular levels the axiomatic character of what was once a mere hypothesis. All outcomes are consequence.

Note that the butterfly does not intentionally cause the tornado. The flap of the wings is part of the initial conditions; one set of conditions leads to a tornado while the opposite set of conditions doesn't. So is with design. It's possible that the set of conditions without the butterfly flapping its wings is the set that leads to a tornado. So is with the spider and its web, the bee and its hive, and the ant and its hill. This can also be seen as a small manner of touching at once (immediate touching) in a vast system apparently unrelated but quite interrelated upon close examination. The work of Edward O. Wilson mentioned before comes up again to insist upon a unity of knowledge (concilience) that unifies the whole regardless of the intentional separations and narrow distinctions arts and sciences might want to establish and maintain. In addition, the HERA (Haddon Electron Ring Accelerator) became the largest particle accelerator in DESY (Deutsches Elektronen-Synchroton) that has enabled probing of the inner workings of the proton. Its work was concluded in 2007 and analysis of findings is still ongoing. These findings and the ability to seek them are exciting but do not suggest that the smallest particles exists wholly outside and independent of the larger particles that contain them. The critical error in physics as well as design rests upon the supposition that the small is independent of the large and can live independently in a self contained whole. On a more complex scenario we can consider the linkages of causality between corporeal, mental and spiritual entities. What extraordinary networks of connectivity and dependability exist hidden from plain view. How much touching is necessary to discover them? How many butterflies are there? The body of landscape architecture has no life outside its boundaries without the context and content of the core.

Crossing wheatfields in Gascogne across softly undulating terrain was a radically different experience than traversing woods in steep and wet slopes while descending from the vicinity of the Massif

Central. The tunnel like view of the woods obscured the view of the NEAR and forced a concentration on the NOW, if for no other reason than to avoid a fall. As a 64 year old, the idea of falling on rock or even sand was not a desirable option and led to a greater or expanded qualitative examination of terrain whereby topography, geology, hydrology, and other earth and natural sciences rushed to the mind with a few dashes of physics and chemistry to encourage greater awareness. It was then possible to observe the textures and contemplate the run of water eroding softer surfaces and pooling debris in low bowls. Over the centuries, the work of running water had cut deeply in some areas to make walking somewhat more challenging. Small habitats (hammocks?) of mosses and short ferns had emerged at these points to create a green carpet full of life that also showcased some flowers and fresh seedlings of larger trees. Explaining this beauty in several languages to fellow walkers made me special for a few moments but also reminded me of some practical applications of the unity of knowledge. The experience on the wheatfields was different. The ground was dry and sandy to make walking more pleasant despite the hard solar slap on the back and neck. The terrain just flowed up and down and sideways and it was possible to see the path undulating and curving lazily ahead. The sky was big and full of color tonalities. However, distance perception was altered by color of air and ground elements along with undulations in the terrain. A city in the distance emerged as tips from steeples or castle turrets apparently close that excited the pace but proved to be farther away than expected. Eventually the path arrived to the base of a larger hill with a city above. The exhausted pilgrim legs had to engage an upward walk (fighting gravity's pull) that often took the last reserve of energy. Centuries ago (for defensive purposes) cities were built on higher ground, either natural or man-made but to a walking pilgrim these defenses became unwitting offenses. A hostel with a shower or a fountain with cool water became magnificent rewards after several hours of marching. So is with the BEYOND. The clarity of getting there provides satisfaction and knowledge that refreshes but there is a price to pay and much knowledge to exchange.

3.- A Change in Extension

The design effort taken as a pilgrimage of the senses forces a change in extension. This is to say that the pilgrim (designer) moves to a location of being (extension) far from the usual and larger in its dimension. This change is not simply a temporary condition but a progressive change across life. This is caused by the accumulation of experience (comprehension) that takes place along the path and the journey. As challenges emerge on the path by physical, mental or spiritual reasons, changes also emerge in person and perception that affect design (journey) outcomes. How those changes are incorporated (made personal) determines the dimensions of the extension. In walking every day, some basic needs of food and refreshment become necessary. The unfamiliarity with local supply sources promoted "extensive" exploration of guides and interaction with local residents and entities. The customary hours of operation for grocery stores, restaurants, markets, and commerces had to be known daily as well as for holidays and weekends. As the daily walk unravelled, there was a parallel search for provisions that would supply the needs of the evening as well as those of the next day. Purchase decisions were made not only on cost but also on weight that would not excessively tax the walking backpacks. Among all needs, drinking water was the greatest. Consumming about one gallon of water per person per day meant carrying 8.6 lbs in suitable liter or half-liter bottles. Trying to drink little water to avoid the weight load was apt to cause dehydration with grave consequences. On some particularly hot days, the water supply was exhausted before arriving at the stage destination and a search for sources overtook the journey as it happened before arriving at Chapel St. Roch where a centenary fountain greeted us after a long march without water. Nothing tasted better that day. The rewards of finding enough supplies is transfered to the design search for data and analysis. Successful outcomes are based on sufficient analytical support (critical thinking) from all sources.

Scales and Proportions

While physical pain and metabolic conflict affect the journey, the largest conflict emerges from topography and climate. Every route looks great on plans and guidebooks. Some even inspire awesome pictures. All become painful on real time and real ground. The importance of on-ground evaluations relates directly to outcome success by connection to reality. On the ground, scale and proportion are real rather than imagined or intellectual. They are not what we want them to be but rather what they are. No amount of intellectual argumentation can flatten a slope or dry a slippery track with sharp rocks and uneven surface. We can talk unceasessly about condition and equipment, but real people need to place real feet connected to real will in order to conquer topography and distance. The distance from St. Jean Pied de Port to Roncesvalles is just a few inches in the map (24 km = 14.4 miles) but the change in elevation is huge (1267 m = 4181.1 ft) yet not imposible to transit. Napoleon and Charlemagne moved their armies up these hills and thousands of pilgrims walked for 6 to 8 hours to reach the hostal. A similar situation occurs later on in the Camino at O Cebreiro on the border mountains to Galicia. The topography challenges and dominates. The legs falter and the only resource is strength of spirit (commitment) very much like the late night hours in the studio before a deadline. From the top of Roncesvalles or O Cebreiro, the land resembles a blanket of green patches and a few rivulets. It is all very romantic and inspiring but the feet and the legs know and remember. The beauty of the landscape distracts from the harshness of the climb along with the spiritual comfort of fulfillment. The path is hard of itself but the context elevates the spirit and provides a greater and more detailed view of the surrounding country. The Basque country and Galicia spread downhill toward a horizon of clouds and evergreens that belie the real condition of humans and institutions as well as history. Fierce battles for control and identity have been fought for centuries in these tender lands. Illusions like these intermingle with design criteria and affect outcomes. This is why inquiry based on truth is critical to successful design outcomes. Historical and cultural research cannot be done without a sincere critical eye that avoids sentimentality and fashionable veils of class, race and gender. Integrity (honesty) is the best research aid. There is no substitute for it.

Perceiving and Recording and Acting

A great advantage of walking the land is the ability and facility to record impressions and data that otherwise might go unnoticed from the reading of topographic, vegetation, cadastral or soil maps. This direct contact is superior to aerial photography or fast touring by automobile. It places the observer in direct proximity that uses all senses. It is not so much the coordinates of place but also the sounds, colors, smells, textures that together provide a fuller picture. The walking approach is probably slow by current standards but quite necessary by design standards. Seeing is a developable skill as much as drafting and sketching. While topographic maps can provide good data on the physical character of the land, it is only by walking that slope and distance can be felt and experienced in true time. In addition, the sensual experience of light, color, texture, smell, sound, and climate is absent from both maps and photographs. The need for actually being there cannot be emphasized enough. In this, design becomes a full contact activity with all the obvious and hidden consequences.

4.- Synthesis of Sensing

The experience of 66 days on the Camino is diverse and complex yet synthetic. There is a constant distillation of experience being transformed into knowledge akin to thickening of a sauce. From the top of mountains, the land blends into color tonalities that remove human and natural presence. The vineyards of La Rioja near Pamplona are quite different from the wheatfields of Gascogne as much as the "correidoras" in Galicia are vastly different from the cow trails in the Aubrac although both are framed by stone walls. Perhaps the cows speak only the local language and their impertubable glances betray an ardent curiosity about far lands and grasses. Each day on the path brings a fresh experience that is digested over time as if it were flowing through a bovine stomach system. Medieval villages hanging from cliffs (Conques, St. Cirq Lapopie) and centenary cathedrals hanging from history (Leon, Burgos, Santiago) speak of a past that will not pass as much as stone "horreos" (granaries) of Galician farmers or stone barns of French farmers. The cliffs that frame the Valley of the Lot river in Haute Loire challenge the flat vastness of the Spanish "meseta" and the rocky coast of Finisterre. It is all part of the large volume of on-field research findings that makes progressive sense and then challenges all sensuality to clarity and renovation. Each design engagement makes the world new again and probably renews us as well.

In the synthesis of experience there are dangers that cause either delays or chases away from the path as well as the inclusion of error very much like in any garden despite all efforts to keep it weed free. Two major problems occur. One is the occlusion effect and the other can properly be called the percussion effect. One relates to position while the other engages perception. Either one poses critical danger.

The Occlusion Effect

The name derives from a meteorological phenomena whereby a cold air mass overtakes a warm front to lift warm air and cause cold weather action to sit stationary with prolonged periods of cold rain and/or snow. In the design research atmosphere, the occlusion caused by poor or insufficient information inflated by emotion or tender heartness results in an incomplete outcome due to data suppression and a suspension of work energy that some students call "brain cramp". Well directed sensorial databases are suddenly lifted away from direct experience and kept aloft while erroneous or false sensitivities are exposed. A precipitating cause for this phenomena is an over sensitizing of issues and direction over minor or secondary matters. The edges of the path offer many and rich temptations for side trips of no import. The removal of the decision making base from the mind to the heart causes a major shift of attention that distracts from the destination. In simple terms "occlusion" represents a rabbit trail that appears attractive in the beginning and ends up causing unnecessary loss of time and focus, unless its stationary condition can be used with profit for further inquiry or reflection. On the way from Navarrete to Najera the trail crosses through vineyards (tempranillo grape for Rioja wine) with sandy, soft soil. After 8km (2 hours) there is the Alto de San Anton right after the village of Ventosa. The wind blows rather strongly but warmly by reason of the North African (Saharan) heat fronts that elevate temperatures above 100 degrees by mid morning. Perspiration is heavy and soon one feels the feet getting moist and rubbing against the socks despite the liberal application of skin protector at the beginning of the daily walk. The cafe in Ventosa is a welcome sight and a popular station for resting before the climb. The burning on the base of the feet becomes stronger and after removal of socks, a blister formation is discovered and treated with desensitizing spray (Novocaine). All is apparently well and the march resumes. Every morning thereafter the blister receives special attention with desensitizing spray, as well as, protective gel and a change of socks halfway in each daily journey. Everything seems to be under control except for the apparently minor yet increasing disturbance of foot pain. Three days later after a rather uncomfortable walk of 12 km to Villafranca Montes de Oca (cobblestoned streets) just before another long climb to the Alto de La Pedraja near San Juan de Ortega, the blister becomes infected and prevents further walking. A time of rest is then forced that enabled a wonderful evening conversation on local history and traditions with a hostel owner and the suggestion of a bus ride to Burgos where medical care of quality is available. Frustrated by the change of mobilization and still underestimating the character and extent of the blister there is a journey of regret across the Montes de Oca (Wilderness of Oca) and a sense of defeat on arrival at the bus terminal in Burgos. At the emergency wing of the university hospital, treatment is swift and kind.

The Seven Da Vinci Principles:

Curiosita: An insatiably curious approach to life.

Dimonstratzione: A commitment to test knowledge through experience.

Sensazione: The continual refinement of the senses, especially sight, as the means to clarify experience.

Sfumato: A willingness to embrace ambiguity, paradox, and uncertainty.

Arte/Scienza: The development of the balance between science and art, logic and imagination ("whole-brain thinking").

Corporalita: The cultivation of ambidexterity, fitness, and poise.

Connessione: A recognition and appreciation for the connectedness of all things and phenomena; "systems thinking."

Michael Gelb. **How to Think Like Leonardo da Vinci: Seven Steps to Genius Every Day**. Dell. 2000

Howard Gardner. **Frames of Mind: The Theory of Multiple Intelligences.** Basic Books. 1983

—————————————.
Intelligence Reframed: Multiple Intelligences for the 21st Century. Basic Books. 2000
——————————. **Multiple Intelligences: New Horizons in Theory and Practice.** Basic Books. 2006
——————————. **Truth, Beauty, and Goodness Reframed: Educating for the Virtues in the Age of Truthiness and Twiter.** Basic Books. 2011

The blister is disinfected and treated with competence. The pain ceases almost immediately and walking becomes pleasurable again. There is a recommended 4 day period of healing that forces an unplanned longer stay at Burgos. Unbeknownst to us the city is celebrating the ten day long Feast of St. Peter. (Los Sampedros). The longer stay at Burgos enabled both the enjoyment of the feast and a more detailed observation of the city, its history, and context. The occlusion effect of the blister front had resulted in a quiet time of reflexion that delivered additional knowledge and enriched the journey. Of course, occlusion fronts are not always beneficial and care must be exercised to prevent derailments of mission and loss of focus.

The Percussion Effect

Another danger in the journey upon the path is the percussion effect that causes disorientation and data conflicts quite similar to echo in a cavern. It is often the result of diverse data streams (echoes) seeking validation and importance by reason of position or volume. The walk across France was rather pastoral and very conducive to reflexion with few fellow pilgrims on the path and no major urban centers to cross. In Spain the path was more urban related as it went across cities and suburbs along with increasing density of walkers after León. The arrival to Santiago was akin to a grand parade made somewhat overwhelming by the narrow streets and the multidirectional walk of the crowd. It seemed as if all the spiders had met at this point to put the finishing touches to their webs. The week before arriving at Santiago presented a Camino filled with excited masses of people chatting, singing, making all manner of noise contrary to the quiet loneliness of previous stages. The maintenance of focus became a constant labor as well as the control of anxiety, as mileage markers kept proclaiming the decreasing distance to the cathedral. It was quite reminiscent of the final stages of a design project when the immediacy of the deadline accelerated the flow of ideas and congested their articulation. A point of making or becoming fruitful that is complicated by the assortment of fruit options (imagine a pear tree able to produce also apples, peaches, and bananas). The much expected synthesis in order seemed to seek disorder or divergence rather than convergence. How to quiet the noise and stay on path and on task?

The recommended solution to occlusion and percussion resides in a symphonic or tonal convergence that puts order in sound as well as in other sensorial elements. This is not an easy task since the convergence might appear as an imposition that deprives senses

Marcus Aurelius. **Meditations**. Penguin. 1964

Richard McKeon (ed). **The Basic Works of Aristotle**. Modern Library. 2001

Ken Robinson. **Out of Our Minds: Learning to be Creative**. Capstone. 2001

_____. **The Element: How Finding your Passion Changes Everything**. Penguin. 2009

Anne Colby, Thomas Ehrlich, Elizabeth Beaumont, Jason Stephens. **Educating Citizens: Preparing America's Undergraduates for Lives of Moral and Civic Responsibility.** Jossey-Bass (Wiley). 2003

of freedom to do and to be. The error in this view of freedom rests in the presumption of order as a limiting factor rather than an enabling mechanism. The focusing of the walk on the path demands a certain amount of order that prevents loss of direction. In academia, the enshrinement of freedom within an occluded notion of "rights" makes both learning and teaching practically impossible unless mentor (teacher) and student develop a symbiotic relation of trust and profit focused upon a larger goal. It is quite impossible to herd cats as it is to teach design thinking to minds and spirits in bodies that have been immersed in easy notions of self-worth and independence from correction. The disciples of the Renaissance masters might not have achieved equal or better greatness, but passed on to posterity the fundamentals of life and skill development that were later used by other generations for their own success. Fundamentals based on discipline that covered not only skill development but also life in all its facets as a regime for success. From the development of perceptive skills to the nourishment of body and mind with proper food, reading, and music. Gelb discusses this topic extensively in his bestseller *"How to Think Like Leonardo da Vinci"* that is supported further by the extensive work of Howard Gardner (Professor of Cognition and Education at Harvard) on intelligence development. Neither Gelb nor Gardner endorse self-indulgence, indolence, truculence (truthiness), obstuseness, and self-esteem pursuit (twittering) as fundamental to or coexistential with talent development. The most recent (2011) work of Gardner ("Truth, Beauty, and Goodness Reframed") extends and underlines the renaissance of virtue education that was preceded by the heralding work of Anne Colby and others under the auspices of the Carnegie Foundation for the Advancement of Teaching on *"Educating Citizens: Preparing America's Undergraduates for Lives of Moral and Civic Responsibility".* In addition, Ken Robinson had followed his very successful presentation in TED with work on creativity based on facts rather than fiction. Their views of "genius" (character) development are not different than those of Aristotle (Ethics) or Marcus Aurelius (Meditations) several centuries before this "Common Era". Thus, the journey on the path of design is guided by well supported precedent that calls for development of vocation and skills particular to each designer yet common to all in a being-and-becoming action. There is no shortcut.

Orchestral Means
and Understandings

Symphonic Principles/Derivative
Practices

What can be said after all? Are pathways of design concurrent with walking paths? Is there concurrency and consilience between them? Can walking provide a better base for land analysis? Can spiders, butterflies, ants, and bees have any true bearing on creative events or are they merely images of possibility? Is our intellectual self truly different and separate from our spiritual and emotional self? Can design be best pursued in neutral and sterilized media (Petri dish) away from direct contact or context? How far is the proper distance between designer and object? These and many more questions emerge and most can probably be dismissed as intellectually insufficient or non peer worthy in reviewability, content, and intent. After all, a historical pilgrimage route can be determined by those who pursue serious inquiry to have no bearing upon the higher pursuit of land design, even if such route bears upon culture and is causative of current conditions. There are boundaries to maintain. The "owners of truth" who have been empowered to lead proper scholarly discussion and inquiry seem to be not only zealous but egotistical about their hard fashioned concepts and constructs. To them, access to knowledge is a perquisite to be properly earned and subjected to filtration rather than open exposure. Yet, there is in all a persistent and insistent ignorance about the rather inconvenient fact that technology and speed of communications have altered the publication landscape in favor of greater agility and freedom. The original purpose of publishing was the facilitation of exchange of ideas rather than the sustenance of the *status quo*. It ihas been argued during the last half of the 20th century that there is only one accepted way to publish and peer review is the approval mechanism of choice. It is rather odd that the peer review system began as an effort to guarantee idoneity and promote collegiality; but, soon morphed into a control mechanism to further only the "approved" ideas and negate divergent thought. Free and open publication is anathema to the peer establishment and validation by "review" becomes a powerful instrument of control not only in the natural and social sciences but also in design. A few publishing venues control the market and books and journals fail to reach their intended audience by reason of price and lateness of arrival.

Large publishers now own most journals and demand access fees or high cost subscriptions to permit access to information thus reducing or causing atrophy in the circles of interest and dialogue. To these barriers must be added the increasing cost of textbooks and instructional materials that effectively substracts students from the major flow of instructional information and pushes them to seek other means (internet based) to obtain learning materials. Like in all controlled environments, there is always a fail-safe or escape route. In our times, the advent of digital on-demand publication that engages the market directly in agile and timely manner has emerged as a way around the fences and filters. Independent publishing is hard to control as it recombines with other forms and meets market demands with greater efficiency and lower costs. The advance time for review and approval deemed necessary for "formal" publication has practically disappeared in the digital environment. The reading public in fiction, scientific andf non-fiction genres is increasingly acclimated to a a faster exchange and a larger selection of topics and treatments. Social networks acts as *de facto* peer reviewers and the number of hits on blogs determine the level of engagement rather than the long and ponderous reviews of a few "peers". The time continuum has shrunk and it might well be also that the creative momentum has increased. The BEYOND has become the NOW.

Yet, design does not exist solely in the BEYOND. The creative urgency has endowed every portion of the path from NOW to NEAR with design content, immediately accessible knowledge and truth that work well under new digital speeds to create a high speed cosmic union under which all portions have validity and meaning in nanoseconds rather than days and weeks. The dimensions of information content have grown from simple Kb files just 20 years ago to Tb size monsters that require not only large storage capacities but faster evaluation mechanisms both technically and humanly. Motion perception and speed of perception have surmounted the domain of visual neuroscience to become a concern for the design disciplines and a current bane in academia. At higher speeds of travel and information sharing fresh scenarios of reality perception (Paul Virilio) are now operative that supercede traditional parameters. Place has become telemetric and fast moving along electronic media (Joshua Meyrowitz) and social networks. Where once a single traffic controller was able to direct the flow of information, now it has become impossible to even understand the meteor shower flashing around us. The BEYOND has become larger and it well could be that it becomes the NEAR.

Paul Virilio. **The Vision Machine**. Indiana. 1994

_____.**The Aesthetics of Disappearance.** Semiotext(e). 2009

_____. **War and Cinema: The Logistics of Perception.** Verso. 2009

Joshua Meyrowitz. **No Sense of Place: The Impact of Electronic Media on Social Behavior.** Oxford. 1985

ANTONIO

She that is queen of Tunis; she that dwells

Ten leagues beyond man's life; she that from Naples

Can have no note, unless the sun were post—

The man i' the moon's too slow—till new-born chins

Be rough and razorable; she that—from whom?

We all were sea-swallow'd, though some cast again,

And by that destiny to perform an act

Whereof **what's past is prologue**, what to come

In yours and my discharge.

William Shakespeare
The Tempest, Act II Scene I:

Design is then the totality of the journey at any speed rather than the controlled locus of a destination. One begins in design, walks in design and arrives in design at design speed. This urgency demands not only skill but also intellectual force that makes decisions concurrent with speed of data input and awareness. Walking on the Camino might apear to be a sloggish trek; however, the amount of data bytes received at each step exceeds the ancient pilgrimage input speed by reason of connection to a larger universe that is increasingly more accessible across time and distance (globalization). The 10th century now (more than ever) speaks to the 21st century with increasing urgency and currency. The thoughts of the moment are transmitted in digital networks right upon conception rather than at a certain future time subject to approval screens (i.e.: totalitarian societies). From the meseta in Spain, I could dial up relatives and friends in USA and South America in real time rather than requesting future time reservations from an operator and waiting hours for a connection as it was the norm just 30 years ago. The physical dimension of the Earth has not changed but its perceptive dimension has shrunk. In a similar manner, response time to ideas is also immediate and thus a high speed dialogue emerges to transcend means and place. It might also be that the notions of place are also altered. We might be one in the cosmos rather than in a locality. In a manner of thinking, design becomes truly universal. This idea is hard to transact in reality by reason of the pace of our human and cultural allegiances that reside far behind the BEYOND and even the NOW.

However, there is more that makes design relevant as well as valent (having valence = a measure of the number of bonds formed by an atom of a given element). That "more" is the humane (quality of being human) content and context. No matter how facinating and bewitching technology can be, the fundamental purpose of design (its locus) is humanity. In this sense, a walk over land and places is apt to extend our human qualities toward a greater understanding of who, what and why we are. The understanding of design has become an orchestral matter that now responds to symphonic principles and practices derived from fresh expressions and consonances. It is a different music for different times and freshly enhanced (perhaps recently invented) instruments. Quite similar to the orchestra in the Chalmun's cantina in Mos Eisley, Tatooine in Star Wars. As it has been said: "The past is prologue" and the real issue is the location and extent of our present time.

True Realities and False Visions

What else can be said? The question posed by professor Malcom Cairns (FASLA) to his students efforts at site analysis echoes tersely across this entire venture: **So, What? . . . . !**

It is not an impertinent expression but rather a keystone to awareness that demands perspicacity (acute mental vision, discernment) beyond the usual answers and formulas. We all know the basic data set and pretend then to have enough information to continue the design journey toward a positive outcome. However, in doing this we ignore particularities and deeper meanings that could provide real significance rather than mere lingo coverage (rhetorical kudzu). In the rush to go from NOW to NEAR, we ignore the context as well as the physiography. In this scenario, all our sites are isolated chunks of land, eerily similar where we impose eerily similar solutions and get praised for use of color . . . No consideration of particulars or extraordinaries can be made since we are in a sensual race toward ourselves rather than toward mankind. This individual isolation is cultivated in design studios and continued in professional practice with greater sophistication than mere earphones and an MP3 player. There is llttle if no inclination to seek information and process it in design form. The dull tones that isolate us in school studios become the high dullness barriers (green walls?) of culture that prevent us from truly seeing and feeling. At some point in the path between high school NOW and college NEAR we have determined that BEYOND is just a concept unnecessary and unreachable. So, it is far better to surrender to the easy path of imitation and accomodation while feigning deep concern for environment and abeyance to its priestly cast. It is far better to remain in the NOW than risk a journey of risk to the NEAR. Somehow the speed of reality overcomes perception and we settle for nostalgia and a bubble of remembrance for what never really was. We might argue vehemently that our place is built in the NOW and will forever stay there (the movie "Groundhog Day"?). That reality is subjective. The realities of Omlsted and Jensen or Church and Kiley are not far from those of Walker, Van Vankelbergh, Corner or even Devigne and Corajoud. Yet, we prefer to live as if 1935 never existed and our vision is a *mélange* of Olmsted Brothers and JJR with a dash of Martha Schwartz. Really, a *pousse-café* cocktail with every ingredient separated by alcoholic density to make a wonderfiul display . . . Along these line we can also see all as *pastiche* (a work that imitates the style of previous work) or as the tango says: a *cambalache* (reciprocal transfer of equivalent sums with different values). It is not a pretty sight; however, the issue is not beauty but vision and cataracts might be rising fast in our lenses.

Of course, there are re-definers (Balmori, Mostafavi, et alii) marking and appropriating small personal plots of ownership and inquiry in a discipline that is far too large and complex for a titanic (titans = Greek mythology) level of dominance. There is in this a reminder of the Treaty of Tordesillas (1494) that divided the known world (western hemisphere) between Spain and Portugal. Subsequently, the Treaty of Zaragoza in 1529 equally divided the eastern hemisphere. The world was simple then, or so all tended to believe. Lost in the simplicity was the complex array of races and cultures and geography between the lines of demarcation that are still being clarified to this day even as the two primary "owners" slide into social and political entropy. Is it possible for landscapoe architecture to be so divided? There is an organic unity (consilience) across time that transcends assigned boundaries (Simon Bell et alii) and mechanisms of control. The profession of landscape architecture (pre and post Olmsted) exists at once in NOW, NEAR and BEYOND ever expanding quite never shrinking or parcelizing. The dominion is vast and the understanding does not yet correspond to the vastness. Of course the Pascalian hypothesis of knowing both large and small by knowing each in turn applies and direct engagements of all dimensions with the land and the culture enable our knowledge and appreciation of the minute and the cosmic that in turn makes our design journey fuller and more complete in all dimensions and in truth. The walk on the Camino was a search for meaning of land and people and culture that somehow transbordered to a discipline and affirmed a pathway for design and life. The journey served well to clarify and to guide and transform. When understood as pilgrimage from NOW to NEAR and BEYOND, design becomes real in a walk that is at once sensual and material, personal and collective.

Symphonies of Perception

There is in the Camino experience a concordance or tonality that speaks of internal and external rhythms. It is a symphonic sound rather than a cacophonic noise. The nuances of each portion of land connect to other nuances to make a collective harmonious

Treaty of Tordesillas
Arquivo Nacional da Torre do Tombo, Portugal and Archivo General de las Indias, Spain

Simon Bell, Ingrid Sarlöv Herlin, Richard Stiles. **Exploring the Boundaries of Landscape Architecture.** Routledge. 2012

Diana Balmori. **A Landscape Manifesto.** Yale. 2010
James Corner. **Recovering Landscape: Essays in Contemporary Landscape Theory.** Princeton. 1999
Gareth Doherty and Mohsen Mostafavi. **Ecological Urbanism.** Lars Müvller. 2010
Charles Waldheim. **The Landscape Urbanism Reader.** Princeton. 2006

sound. They gather to form a symphonic compendium (collection) that expresses continuity as well as stillness in concordance as well as divergence in tonality. In the resulting tensions, there is the emergence of knowledge that guides design action. The Roman and Romanesque bridges in both France and Spain celebrated local needs of commerce and transit as well as a universal vision of empire that invariably and unwittingly served the purposes of pilgrimage and nation building across cultures. Like the stones in the bridges, every part of the walk fits into a complete perceptive whole. The number of steps from Le Puy en Velay to Santiago de Compostela acquire larger significance in their unity. Each step is a vital element of a larger picture. A movement in a symphony.

What then can be derived from this journey? The fruit of a walk of 1,000 miles in 66 days across 2 countries and almost 12 regions can be harvested in seven values. The foundation for values is loosely anchored in Classical Greek philosophy and its eventual pilgrimage through Latin and Renaissance philosophy and governance that is now reflected in practice and cultural undergirdings. Values were after all, just disciplines for the development of habits. A strong fabric of Reformed Christian belief and practice has embedded the values into the culture whether in a sub or supra position. Our minds are not merely "western" by location but stand there by legacy (DNA) even if we cultivate "eastern" tastes and fashions. Quite simply, the cathedrals of Europe do not stand alone and like Cendrars notes: "speak to each other in the night" (*Prose du Transsibérien et de la Petite Jeanne de France*) as much as we speak to each other in our inherited past. People along the length of the Camino bear witness of past and present faith (life) that becomes a philosophical legacy for current practical life. The values stated here are affirmed from personal interaction with culture, lore, and practice through observation, dialogue, and engagement bereft of a formal academic concentration or (alas!) a peer review and approval process. Perhaps, not unlike Job, I sit naked on a pile of dung without inquirIng minds all around except for the inopportune presence of some friends. Of course, dung can fertilize growth and fruit bearing.

By prior knowledge across 65 years of life experience, numerous engagements with people and thinkers, extensive observation of practice mores and multi-lingual connections to authors and practitioners in architecture, planning, and landscape architecture, these values have been honed as a core of life and action. Due to a current assignement of 15 years in academia, the values have a didactic and legacy focus for transmission to students and might not be of great interest to teaching faculty. In essence, these values represent what I am or have become and reflect an affirmation in the walk between Le Puy en Velay and Santiago de Compostela. It is not just 1000 miles in one summer but many thousands of miles in a lifetime.

Most certainly, there has been a review or rethinking of Late Modernism since about 1984 that has affected allegiances to the dominant concepts and precepts of the 19th and 20th century. A dynamic critical reappraisal and repositioning of Early Modern (Kant) and Medieval (Aquinas) philosophy is currently taking place according to my friends vested in philosophy and some refugees of Post-Modernism. The ethical positions of Aristotle and Aquinas are now the subject of animated discussion in a search not only for meaning but also for a point of beginning and purpose for web weaving. The spider senses of the culture are tingling not only in classrooms but in bars, cafes, and kitchen tables across Europe and America. We live now in an age of risk, more so than in previous ages. Some would love to take a risk like a plunge in a cool lake but need assurances of safety. I have no such assurances; however, the following values might help develop strong habits that of themselves can provide the desired measure of safety.

1.- **Value of Intuition:** The affirmation of acquired knowledge and its consistent presence in design as well as in life is guided by intuition. From time inmemorial or at least since 1851 (Great Exhibition in Crystal Palace, London), design is the product of knowledge either recent or past. The Great Exhibition is used as a point at which modern industry began to harvest the fruits of colonization and set in motion the worldwide exchange of goods and services that would eventually make globalizationn possible 150 years later. Vast amounts of knowledge were exchanged that today live in the sub-conscious of the 21st century or in its sanitary landfills.

The argument that design can occur spontaneously; as in *ex nihilo* conditions, neglects to admit the role of the developing mind in human action. From birth (and probably before) man is a creature of experience (knowledge) that reacts to environment and needs from a base of cumulative experience either personal or collective, acquired or inherited. The developmental process of humans

Jonathan W. Schooler, Stellan Ohlson, and Kevin Brooks. *Thoughts Beyond Words; When Language Overshadows Insight"*. Journal of Experimental Psychology. 122. No 2. (1993)
Cited by Gladwell. **Blink**. Ch 4. p119

Malcolm Gladwell. **Blink: The Power of Thinking Without Thinking.** Little, Brown, and Company. 2005

"Generic, epigenetic, and experiential events provide each of us with a unique brain. Each of our brains is skilled at some things and not skilled at others. What those skills are depends on the complex mix of our biology and our experience in the world. Most of us have brains that are very good at some things we all value, things that could serve us well in our lives. These are our gifts.
One of the most basic kinds of change in our brains is the change that builds on what we already have - our neurological gifts. There is no simpler way to learn than to practice things we already know. Synapses get stronger with use"

James E. Zull. **The Art of Changing the Brain: Enriching the Practice of Teaching by Exploring the Biology of Learning**. Stylus. 2002
page 117

(as well as other vertebrates) bears witness to schooling into life through acquisition of basic skills (crawl, walk, talk, feel, see, hear) and their exercise of this knowledge in life and community (Zull, *The Art of Changing the Brain*). By age 12 or so our minds (neuronal networks) are loaded with sufficient intuitive or prior knowledge to survive and we are then able to assess new or current knowledge from that base. At age 26 or so, the synapses (places where signals or information pass from one neuron to another) seem to come together by "epigenetic" processes (caused by physical and cellular events) to promote greater maturity and wider awareness. This "nurturing" process promotes "neuronal change" (knowledge acquisition/experience) that is evident in the areas impacted by change. No design action emanates entirely from current or potential (non-acquired) knowledge. Thus, intuition (previous knowledge or unconcious) plays a major role in design decision processes as either instigator or affirmer. It is critical for designers to have prior knowledge and to enlarge it by continuous and extensive life learning.

Malcolm Gladwell. **Blink.** Little, Brown and Co. (Time-Warner). 2005
E. O. Wilson. **Sociobiology: The New Synthesis.** Belknap Press. 2000

Malcolm Gladwell (*Blink*) notes the value of the adaptive unconscious (prior knowledge bank) in decision making. This is the corrective mechanism of digested knowledge (truth) that keeps direction on the correct path. The progressive accumulation of knowledge enables faster reaction to new and future challenges as well as a more nuanced (better informed) critique of those challenges that leads to the achievement of clarity (truth). It is not a labored or prolonged process because the mental computer (unconscious) has not only deep data memory but also fast operating speed. We have no idea how much we know until it is necessary to show and use it. This is not a new discovery since Plato (424 - 348 BC) had already mentioned it in his dialogues. Following upon the view of Socrates that reality is not only the graspable or touchable but the "invisible", Plato in *Theaetetus* (156a), argues that people who do not see beyond the obvious have no "divine inspiration" (intuition) that gives access to higher insights about reality. These "insights" are based on previous knowledge (inspiration or intuition) fertilized by ideation (collection of ideas/meditation on knowledge). In essence, reality is available only to those who use the senses as illustrated in the *Allegory of the Cave* where the contrast is shown between an invisible yet intelligible world and a visible but less knowledgeable world. The ability to see rather than merely to look is enhanced by intuition. A designer is called to extend the mind backwards and forward and sideways.

Of course, intuition can be bent or altered by cultural perceptions and forcibly acquired or imposed concepts. Humans are social and gregarious beings subject to influence by peerages and cultural currents (religion, philosophy, and science) derived from group selection rather then purely from an evolutionary progress or compulsion beyond control. The balancing elements (checkpoints) in morality, religion, and art are guided by understandings of truth. Upon these rest the human dominance of the Earth. (E. O. Wilson). No matter the complexity of group game schemes, the truth will always emerge (purification process)because the balance of creation (the universe) rests on such a fulcrum. No doubt, this is a controversial issue (sociobiology) now, as it was when Dr. Wilson first proposed it. My aim is far from entering a beehive but to recognize that a beehive exists and it is worth noting its presence and value for design action. Moreover, the spiritual that envelops the universe is not a matter of religion. It is the natural order of things whereby a spider cannot impersonate a bee or a peach tree pretend to be an elm. Creatures both animal and vegetal have no choices about being while enjoying ample room to become all that they can be within natural laws that are somehow inscribed in our intuitive memory banks. Truth holds all things in their infinite schema justs as the orbits of planets or the routing of ant pathways.

Truly, the walk on El Camino would not have been as successful as it was with less information from the knowledge accumulated over a lifetime and its inherent truth. The value for design rises from an appreciation of the value of direction and preparation (planning) based on true knowledge as fundamental to profitable analysis and successful outcomes. In simple terms we can agree with the traditional saying: *"plan the work and then work the plan"* Success cannot rest in nothing less. Serendipity is just the occasional cherry on top rather than the entire sundae delight.

2. Value of Risk: Starting with the notion that anything worth doing is worth doing well, there is a beginning (NOW) that is surrounded by the unknown while encouraged to march forward by intuition (rational and spiritual). At this point a decision is made to trace a path toward the NEAR. This risk might seem foolish to others who lack either courage or trust in their base of intuitive knowledge. In most student studio settings, the risk is masked by various screens proper of both the age and the pedagogy. In professional offices the risk is overcome by notions of value and gain. In both cases, risk entails an action in courage rather than an assured outcome effort. It is avoided by indulgence on its negative aspects (failure probability). The roll of the dice holds an equal number of good and bad probabilities. Choosing not to roll is one of the bad ones.

Over time we grow accustomed to risk-taking as integral to the design action. Gladwell again speaks of acting based on "rapid cognition" as the ability to act without having to explain the action (verbal overshadowing per Schooler). Earlier on I spoke of "muscle memory" which is generally co-equivalent. Of course, not everybody has this capacity or can lead others in the use of this capacity since the instinctive action is to play for safety. Moreover, it is not a readily teachable skill that is more linked to vocation and talent than mere desire to have. It is rational rather than emotional and is supported by the spiritual (whether devoted or secular). The play for safety is the generally accepted coin of the realm. It buys the right to do the true and tried in the high probability of directed and acceptable success. Yet, there is within us sufficient stored information to take a "calculated" risk in search of a larger prize. The spider jumps from precognition rather than upcoming or yet to be acquired knowledge. Many of my students and colleagues pursue the safety of "case studies" as exemplars for the solution of problems rather than cheerleaders (motivators) for the assumption of risk. It is easy to stack five or ten such cases and be comforted in replicative uses of style and technology but it is very hard to translate those cases into a fresh approach or a different pathway of design thinking. In fact, such action is often discouraged by grading processes or time constraints in design phase enforcement. Nevertheless, a leap of risk with cheerleaders all around is preferable to a safe stroll on a clear and flat surface framed by railguards. In these early days of the 21st century we have developed great affection for objective safety in the pursuit of common certainty while surrounded by vast reachable and interactional amounts and speeds of information available in real time that can provide true and exciting safety for leaps of any dimension. It is only in knowledge that we attain true safety. In this I am reminded of an old cartoon that shows a man painting a room (floor and walls) only to find himself trapped at a corner away from the door surrounded by wet paint. Scratching his head, the man then paints a door and exits the room. This capacity for invention arises from rapid cognition. It is a reaction in risk from resources (intuition) rather than a call to a council of consensualization to conceptualize safe approaches to a possible safe solution. Others would sit waiting for the paint to dry or peers to advise as to the safest option. Peers equally afraid to say or do the wrong thing.

The value of risk is defining and definitive in the design enterprise. It needs to be encouraged and cultivated as a basic and distinctive element of a profession that purports to promote healthy outcomes through stewardship of resources. Central Park, New York and Jackson Park, Chicago (F. L. Olmsted) were a huge risk in their time as it is nowadays the High Line, New York(Field Operations), or the Brooklyn Bridge Park, Brooklyn (MVVA) or Fresh Kills, New York (Field Operations) or Stratford City, London (West8) or the Qinhuagdao Red Ribbon Park, China (Turenscape) and many other large and great projects. These projects demanded fresh application of existing knowledge and ample translation of possibilities from extra-disciplinary areas. They are not the work of risk adverse protection and safety seekers, but rather fruits of inquiry and translation by fearless people. Thus, instruction needs to be focused and intensive rather than erratic and cuddling. A good point of beginning can be the selection of students based on a reality of vocation rather than the illusion of dreams or socio-political constructs of equality and justice. Studios need not be crowded with spectators and tinkerers. The attraction of life in a design studio is a powerful motivator; however, gravel needs to be stirred in a pan to reveal the gold nuggets. The journey is for the gold rather than the gravel. Design studios are for design students and need to be populated with young people of talent and promise that can elevate themselves to a transit of consequence on the path rather than crowd it with unnecessary needs and wants. Rigor begins in the selection process just like the flower begins at the roots. The best marathon runners edge toward the front in order to avoid the complicated and dangerous transit jamming action of the less proficient, as well as the distractions of peripheral obstacles. Quite very much like the search flight of bee swarms (Seeley). The profession (as any serious enterprise) cannot become a refugee camp for people injured in other lost journeys or a place to find the reason for being or a convenient fantasy fulfillment camp; but, it is rather a preparation field for serious and definitive engagements in a complex field demanding of courage and invention. Like the camps (fortresses) of Templar Knights, the studio is a preparation arena for engagement in real time with real issues in the daily real life of the territory (discipline). There were other convents, shelters, and abbeys to attend to the needs of those seeking to be healed or comforted in the same way that the U S Marine Corps (Templar

Aristotelian Virtues
Generally defined as a means between two extremes.
A tension condition between good and evil.

Courage
Temperance
Generosity (or liberality)
Pride
Good temper
Truthfulness
Wittiness
Friendliness
Modesty
Righteous indignation

Roman Virtues (Expansion/ adaptation of Aristotle by Seneca, Cicero, Marcus Aurelius, and others to embody the ideal Roman character and conduct. Generally follow or promote a Stoic point of view)

Auctoritas—"Spiritual Authority"—The sense of one's social standing, built up through experience, Pietas, and Industria.

Comitas—"Humour"—Ease of manner, courtesy, openness, and friendliness.

Constantinum—"Perseverance"—Military stamina, mental and physical endurance.

Clementia—"Mercy"—Mildness and gentleness.

Dignitas—"Dignity"—A sense of self-worth, personal pride.

Disciplina—"Discipline"—Military oath under Roman protective law & citizenship.

Firmitas—"Tenacity"—Strength of mind, the ability to stick to one's purpose.

Frugalitas—"Frugalness"—Economy and simplicity of style, without being miserly.

Gravitas—"Gravity"—A sense of the importance of the matter at hand, responsibility and earnestness.

Honestas—"Respectability"—The image that one presents as a respectable member of society.

Humanitas—"Humanity"—Refinement, civilization, learning, and being cultured.

Industria—"Industriousness"—Hard work.

Iustitia—"Justice"—Sense of moral worth to an action.

Pietas—"Dutifulness"—More than religious piety; a respect for the natural order socially, politically, and religiously. Includes the ideas of patriotism and devotion to others.

Prudentia—"Prudence"—Foresight, wisdom, and personal discretion.

Salubritas—"Wholesomeness"—Health and cleanliness.

Severitas—"Sternness"—Gravity, self-control.

Veritas—"Truthfulness"—Honesty in dealing with others.

Knights) cannot be the Emergency Room of the local hospital. Certainly, this will sound harsh to many and I will be castigated for intemperance and incorrect thinking; however, my experience of 40 plus years in practice and 15 in teaching have shown me quite clearly that my teaching function is eventually reduced to the 10% to 20% of students that are genuinely committed to the discipline rather than the 10% wholly unfocused and the 60% to 80% softly engaged in a tinkering or sampling expedition as in a trip to a dinner buffet or a movie rental store. Yet, every semester the starting line is crowded with indiscriminate masses that are not refined by a competitive effort until mid semester. It is still true that silk purses cannot be made from sows ears no matter the amount of instructional and counseling efforts or the technological candy that can be offered. It is not a matter of pedagogy or "nurturing" but rather of true talent and passion. The outcomes of teaching (mentoring) by the masters of the High Renaissance (Michelangelo, Leonardo, Raphael) produced mediocre artists probably because there was not in them a true vocational drive but only an attraction (infatuation) to prominence. Kind of a social imperative for group membership. In a sense, they were "groupies" as much then as today. The design studio needs time and space for the truly committed as much as the science lab needs true scientists and scholars.

3.- **Value of Spirit**: In academia more than in general society, the spiritual value in design is discounted in favor of an assumed neutrality that is more antinomial than nominative The issue is not a religious one and really not a matter of faith expression. It is simply an issue of humanity in its fullest dimension. Tri-dimensional beings (mind/body/soul) need to work in all dimensions to sustain their true being. No single dimension exists without the other nor can be expressed individually alone (three-legged stool effect). Design as a human expression needs to be accessible to all dimensions of the beings that will use and enjoy it. Park benches and trees are not neutral elements. They reflect both the cosmos and a concern for wellness as well as the intelligence (knowledge) of a designer. Thus, the consideration of spiritual content needs to be integral to any design task or pursuit. The geometric rigor of Parc André Citröen in Paris by Gilles Clément would be just a vain material exercise without the spiritual content of community, celebration, and remembrance. For that matter the Jardin des Tuileries next to the Place de la Concorde (Place de la Révolution) where the guillotine was once located, would be just a bunch of trees and

"I wanted to understand how people could listen to Haydn, Mozart, and Beethoven one day and beat up the Jews the next"

Eric Kandel. **The Age of Insight: The Quest to Understand the Unconscious in Art, Mind, and Brain, from Vienna 1900 to the Present.** Random House. 2012

_____. **In Search of Memory: The Emergence of a New Science of Mind.** W W Norton. 2007

Edward O. Wilson. **Sociobiology: The New Synthesis.** Belknap Press. 1975/2000

_____. **The Social Conquest of Earth**. Liveright/W. W. Norton and Company. 2012

_____. **Biophilia**. Harvard. 1984

chairs on a plane of grass and gravel if it were not for its context both current and historical. The life that permeates both places is not artificial matter or intellectual construct. It is real. People sit or play or love in real time while feeling joy, weather, beauty, sexuality, air, color, texture, sound, history, and many more emotions and things proper of humans. Moreover, they also remember. No discussion of nothingness or absence of being applies. The places exist to validate and celebrate the human spirit across and in time. Spirit as the living force of the universe rather than a dry concept of constructed celestial mechanics. The spirit is free energy in content and context that emanates solely from the reality of being human. Issues of theology and faith structure can be concurrent but the critical determinant is freedom. It is not an assignation (directed location in time and place) but a real presence that transcends like the aroma in the ovary of the flower or the blastula at the cleavage of the zygote.

Freedom can be simply expressed as the condition of not being captive. Certainly, the pretense at intellectuality, moral neutrality and truth holding (ownership) is attractive and can exert power and influence that often regulates content and direction in themes and outcomes. However, this pretense only produces narrow lives of mind and body poor in spiritual energy that serve only to crate (package or box) narrow people in dimensionally similar boxes. Design is a liberator and the spirit sustains its liberating action. The limitations of expression in the Soviet Union (1922 - 1991) served to create sterile non-humane urbanism and landscape as well as a national sense of despair (morass) that could not be obviated by scientific or sports achievements. The unqualified and unbridled contamination of the environment, as well the promotion of a culture of egotism and envy became the legacy of a materialistic (non-spiritual) system that is now suffering the dire consequences of parcelization and constraining of the human condition along with an intentional or doctrinal spoilage of nature and its resources. By contrast, a corresponding ideological system in China is now engaged in a massive environmental clean-up under pressure from expanding needs of people for a better living place (standard of living) that is not solely based on the attainment of material goods but rather freedom of spirit in open space (parks and such). The human and ecological dimension of current major projects of landscape architecture in China bear witness to this development. In this we might note the large number of Chinese students pursuing advanced degrees in landscape architecture (MLA and PhD) supplemented by the number of American and European design teams and firms now providing design consultation and project execution services across China. It could be inferred that landscape architecture flourishes and is most effective in freedom (spirit) based or seeking environments.

4.- Value of Mind: When we consider the Olympic ideal of *Mens Sana in Corpore Sano* the issue of sanity emerges. It is not so much about mental illness but rather about balance of intellectual and physical purpose. It is about the wider scope of the brain beyond the collection and processing of data or the body as the holder of life. To some it is neurobiology while for others it is simply memory. In landscape architectural practice, the role and value of memory is rather all encompassing and essential. Whether for existential purposes or simply as a celebratory gesture, memory acts to connect dots, underline events, create metaphors, expand meaning, infuse depth, order history, celebrate origin, encourage celebration, and many other humanly possible things. The spaces we create are mnemonic devices of various tones and scales that often go beyond single locations and events to become universal. A simple statue atop a mountain becomes a symbol of city, country and culture as with the statue of Cristo Redentor (Christ Redeemer) atop Corcovado overlooking the harbor of Rio de Janeiro. It goes beyond religious instrument to become an iconic and transcendent element far more prominent than the Tijuca tropical forest around it or the Tijuca favela that hangs below it. A steel tower on the banks of a river was intended to showcase technology and became an identity giver and cultural landmark, as with the Eiffel Tower in Paris or the 10-story Vijay Stambha tower in Chittorgarh Fort in Rajasthan, India. Of course, memory is not solely prompted by large and powerful icons. In daily life we encounter parks, boulevards, and small gardens that trigger not only good feelings but memories that enrich and enlarge life. Eric Kandel (Nobel Prize, 2000) founder of the Center for Neurobiology and Behavior at Columbia University survived the horror of Kristallnacht (1929) and the emerging Nazi regimen to emigrate to USA and become the foremost memory expert in our time. His work on the biology of memory liberated memory from psychoanalysis and Marxist dialectic and placed it in neurobiology (*In Search of Memory*, 2006/*The Age of Insight*, 2012) with consequent greater understanding and engagement by ancillary and parallel disciplines. Alongside Kandel's work runs the lifelong effort of E. O. Wilson and his development of *Sociobiology* (1975). This translation (movement) of memory to biology away

"This new science is based on five principles. First, mind and brain are inseparable . . . Second, each mental function in the brain - from the simplest reflex to the most creative acts in language, music, and art - is carried out by specialized neural circuits in different regions of the brain . . . . . . Third, all these circuits are made up of the same elementary signaling units, the nerve cells. Fourth, the neural circuits use specific molecules to generate signals within and between nwrve cells. Finally, these specific signaling molecules have been conserved - retained as it were - through millions of years of evolution.

. . . .

Because of its broad implications for individual and social wellbeing, there is now a consensus in the scientific community that the biology of mind will be to the twenty-first century what the biology of the gene was to the twentieth century."
Eric Kandel, **In Search of Memory** *(Preface)*

E. O. Wilson. The Social Conquest of
Earth. Liveright. 2012

"They (Marxist critics) disliked the idea, to put it mildly, that human nature could have a genetic basis at all. They championed the opposing view that the developing human brain is a tabula rasa . . . If genes prescribe human nature, they said, then it follows that ineradicable differences in personality and ability also might exist. Such possibilty cannot be tolerated, said the critics, because it tilts thinking into a slippery slope down which humankind easily descends to racism, sexism, class oppression, colonialism, and - perhaps worst of all - capitalism! As the century closes, this dispute has been settled. Genetically based variation in individual personality and intelligence has been conclusively demonstrated.

. . . .

Among many social scientists and humanities scholars a deeper and less ideological source of skepticism was expressed, and remains. It is based on the belief that culture is the sole artisan of the human mind. This perception is also a tabula rasa hypothesis that denies biology, or at least simply ignores biology. It too is being replaced by acceptance of the interaction of biology and culture as the determinant of mental development.

. . . . .

Since the early nineteenth century it has been generally assumed that the natural sciences, the social sciences, and the humanities are epistemologically disjunct from one another, requiring different vocabularies, modes of analysis, and rules of validation . . . . .

. . . .

from evolution, created a considerable uproar in scientific circles with rather intense opposition from some sectors (Stephen Jay Gould/Richard C. Lewontin) who insisted on a Marxist model where memory was seen as a flat table (*tabula rasa*) subject to the imposition of ideas (indoctrination) rather than a biological process of enrichment and liberation (previous and acquired knowledge encouraged by experience). The triumph of biology has been critical to the development of fresher concepts of memory and its role in various aspects of culture and the arts (landscape architecture among them). As with the path of the design walk, the process Kandel used to reach neurobiology and that of Wilson to reach sociobiology led to many comparisons, immersions, and explorations that supported postulates and connections that served to engage issues such as spatial memory (perception and behavior) along with the role of science in art (and viceversa). In direct exemplification of an inquiring journey, Kandel engaged and synthetized themes from several branches of knowledge to acquire depth of understanding as well as awareness of knowledge width (amplitude). His creation of neurobiology was framed by learning excursions (akin to language acquisition) into medicine, psychiatry, physiology, bio-chemistry, and bio-physics. Each in turn provided linkages to other areas very much in the manner of a spider web. His experience with National Socialism also framed his effort at understanding the role of memory in supporting and promoting behavior (Why do we do what we do?). Along the same lines, E. O. Wilson (minus the Nazi experience) was able to discern the basic character of humans from many webbing journeys across disciplines.

So, design emerges as a fertile field for the practice of liberating inquiry and discovery rather than a flat vehicle of expression for rigid world and social views. It is this freedom that makes the profession look easy and soft on the one hand or hard and complex on the other. Efforts at definition have proven rather slippery or confining., at best. Students and practitioners as well as academics of consequence share in the same total substance and essence that makes the universal body of the discipline, rather than in isolated districts unreferenced to a core. In this context, landscape architecture is always in the process of transplanting itself to larger pots from a deep and powerful memory of itself. Perhaps the profession has a combination of aerial and ground roots that enable a far and wide reach of mind and spirit. The journey to BEYOND follows pathways of mind and spirit that can be diverse as much as they are congruent. The good news is that they flow in freedom rather than assignations of doctrine.

5.- Value of Body: The showcasing of the nutrition habits of high renaissance art masters (Da Vinci, Michelangelo, Raphael) by the worlk of Gelb and others led to a promotion of their diet ("Renaissance Diet" and emulators) as a desirable health alternative to combat the physical ailments of modern man. Somehow, the daily regime of cereal potage, bean soup and the attendant bread and wine was supposed to promote better health and more creative (satisfying) life. While the diet might be profitable for the care of the physcal body, it might not be so for extensions of the body like presence and expression. There is more to the body than consumption of food, proper elimination, and maintenance of figure. The diet of the masters included a set of habits of exercise, conduct (presence), garment fitting, self awareness, image projection, and civic manners (behavior in community). When Lawrence Halprin spoke of movement, he invariably referred to choreographed dance (Nicollet Mall, Ira Keller Fountain, Freeway Park) rather than merely a body shaking experience. The idea was to promote meaningful movement in and through the design object as well as in the perception and body of the viewer.

The solution to the problem now evident is the recognition that the line between the great branches of learning is not a line at all, but instead a broad, mostly unexplored domain awaiting cooperative exploration from both sides."

Edward O. Wilson. **Sociobiology: The New Synthe sis.** Preface to 25th Anniversary Edition, 2

A concept of the body that embraces the virtues (Aristotle and others), also of necessity will embrace a dominant expression of bonhomie = good manship = cordiality that envelops all actions public and private. This is the cornerstone of true design success focused upon service to others rather than personal prominence. Design being at its core a concrete expression of service. By this concept, it is possible to establish a climate of access and participation to person and mind that facilitates understanding of mission as well as education of client and society. There is in every design outcome and process a didactic element that elevates and enriches community. Thus, the well cared body extends to expression and action in concert with knowledge and skills to the benefit of community (public service) that invariably will be reflected in gains of esteem for the designer. For Leonardo, the issue was not so much the attire but the manner of personal conduct free from affectation. The Seven Da Vinci Principles identified by Gelb mirror the Aristotelian and Roman Virtues to emphasize the need for practical and constant (enduring) standards. Of course, for a few decades, the concept of virtue has been altered and even eliminated from discourse and practice. The personalization and

The Seven Da Vinci Principles:

Curiosita: An insatiably curious approach to life.

Dimonstratzione: A commitment to test knowledge through experience.

Sensazione: The continual refinement of the senses, especially sight, as the means to clarify experience.

Sfumato: A willingness to embrace ambiguity, paradox, and uncertainty.

Arte/Scienza: The development of the balance between science and art, logic and imagination ("whole-brain thinking").

Corporalita: The cultivation of ambidexterity, fitness, and poise.

Connessione: A recognition and appreciation for the connectedness of all things and phenomena; "systems thinking."

Michael Gelb. **How to Think Like Leonardo da Vinci: Seven Steps to Genius Every Day**. Dell. 2000

Howard Gardner. **Truth, Beauty, and Goodness Reframed: Educating for the Virtues in the Twenty-First Century**. Basic Books. 2011m

isolated individualization of human conduct apart from a common social compact has promoted antinomian attitudes that have proven deleterious to common harmony and happiness (consider Greece's financial default or Occupy movements). Recently, an effort has been made politically and philosophically at refocusing the discussion and didactic exposition of virtue as a means to recover community vision and strength. The scrutiny of classical virtues in light of current failures of individually defined morality emerges as a convenient handrail to guide a possible ascent out of Plato's cave. To this effect, Howard Gardner offers a re-study of truth, beauty, and goodness as a means to a meaningful engagement with the age (21st century). As stewards of the Earth (Nature), landscape architects need to em-body virtue to add a compelling force to their labors.

6.- Value of Craft: In teaching drawing to first year design students, there is always the question of better approaches or techniques. The usual hand drawing approach now appears too old and plainly too difficult to master. It demands far more discipline than students are willing to employ or that teachers are prepared to instruct. New systems and digital applications tempt students to focus upon a quick outcome of representation skill rather than a communication effort. A vague rationalization about the better use of time to pursue other curricular attractions, is often employed for the abandonment of hand and mechanical drawing. In the tension between representation and communication, there is a territory of purpose that goes wholly unexplored (ignored). This territory contains the development of craft that affirms skill and supports thinking, creativity and representation. The triangulation of eye, hand and mind is abandoned for the sake of a mechanical approximation distant from both the producer and the product as well as alien to the public. It is akin to an avoidance of thought for the sake of doing something free of mental rigor that can only generate a transitory good feeling. Under these conditions, an increasing number of graduates, both bachelor and master level have managed to cruise through programs avoiding the currents of craft developmen in drawing. PhD candidates often are illiterate about history and graphic communication but aspire to a managerial role in design firms or a tenure track refuge in academia. Design proficiency in their case is downgraded to elaborate rhetorical statements with dashes of philosophical content that is intended to atone for the absence of design proficiency. Bachelor and Master graduates manage to engage the practice and learn on the job while

PhD candidates follow pathways increasingly farther removed from the disciplinary core and mission to the detriment of the profession. It is not about credentials alone but also about competence and capability along with skillful communication.

Like a language, graphic representation capability is fundamental to design communication. Unfortunately, advanced levels of graphic application wizardy are insufficient to convey design intent. Very complex arrangements of entourage and reality imitation (BIM, AutoCAD, SketchUp, etc) might delight the senses; but, like empty façades leave a sterile feeling behind that fails to reach the viewer intellectually or emotionally. The result is that professional illustrators are now called to do what designers customarily did in the process of design action and representation. Yet, the illustrators cannot convey the design sentiment. They are merely translators with no concept of content or context or impact or purpose. A public reaction has been building up as an adversion to the perfect, photographic look of illustrations and a demand has emerged for more humane illustrations. This explains to a certain point the popularity of watercolor as a media as well as hand tracing that gives the sensation of human rather than machine treatment. However, our love of technology continues to be expressed in unintelligible renderings alien to the audience and often deleterious to the project. The old way of seeing is grafted far too deeply in humankind to accept new ways of seeing that demand altered senses or states of perception.

What to do? While coming far from suggesting the elimination of digital applications, it is probably useful to school designers in the acquisition of basic skills in drawing that can be supplemented by digital products. There needs to be an insistence in the development of perception from direct hands-on experience rather than arm-length engagement. Eliminate filters of perception that foster a synthetic view of land, man, and community. The idea is one of building a perceptual bridge, that in denoting humane action, can effectively convey a communicable accessible engagement to humans. Of course, it is important for students to be aware and investigate other design aspects or notions but we must be keenly aware of the need to build the core rather than transit on the periphery, unless we want to make pies with beautiful crusts but devoid of content. Air filled pies are better suited to exhibits in appliance displays than as expressions of understanding and direction in design. Drawing the land and diagramming its content, built a substantial base for understanding landscape and culture during the walk on El Camino de Santiago. It fostered a deeper engagement and provided an opportunity for reflection. Many of the notes in this meditation began as handwritten diagrams and concepts in loose pieces of paper that eventually demanded clarification and annotation. The writing at a keyboard in front of a 17 inch screen was not sufficiently immediate. So is with digital drawing applications and their outcomes.

7.- Value of Imagination: During the past 20 years or so there have been claims of a dearth of imagination across the culture that is reflective of various factors social and political, as well as educational. Social conditions have limited speech and idea articulation along rigid lines of conduct and expression. The formalism noted by Marc Treib (*The Content of Landscape Form: The Limits of Formalism*) has evolved rather than devolved into a manner (form) of rigid conformance that dominates design outcomes with a sameness that pretends to pass for creative dynamism. The work of a few professionals like (for example): Dr. Konjian Yu at Turanscape (Tanghe River/Tianjin Qiaoyuan Wetland); Gilles Clement (Parc André Citröen); Allain Provost (Parc Diderot) and Michel Corajoud (Parc de Sausset/Parc de Gerland/Parc des Coudrays) goes a long way to exhibit originality and freshness that contrasts rather strongly with current major works that despite being endowed with ambitious programs and large cultural projection, seem to speak the same narrow and measured language. Whether in New York City, Los Angeles, Chicago, Santa Monica, Seattle, Rotterdam, or London, the design outcomes speak the same language and thematic. At no time in recorded history, have we said more and meant less. There seems to be no creativity in the search and exposition of solutions, the consideration of options, and the enunciation of alternatives. By reason of current fracturization of political and social environments, we have built barriers to free expression that prevent honest and imaginative exploration of verbal, written and spoken communication. We know that without imagination we are not fulfilling our human and cultural potential; but, are prevented by these created barriers from effectively addressing the problem. Poverty of imagination might well be the problem of the age but its solution challenges the constructs that bind us to the status quo. Indeed, the situation is dangerous and prevents improvement of the individual and collective learning process that provides meaning to experience and guides the use and enrichment of knowledge.

Marc Treib. **The Content of Landscape Form (The Limits of Formalism).** Landscape Journal. 20: 2_01. p119-140

Imagination is fundamental to the understanding of the world around us, yet it is increasingly absent from daily experience.

The extant notion that perception depends on worldview was originally supported by the work of Jean Piaget (1896 -1980) on cognitive development and became a standard in developmental psychology with links to pedagogy. Within this framework, the qualitative development of knowledge reaches its height in the development of perception and memory. The resulting world view is a result of the work of imagination in arranging perception (making sense of space). In our times, this essential corollary is increasingly absent from an environment of social coercion dominated by post-modern grievance and social constructs. Under these conditions, the freedom inherent in design expression is suppressed and often eliminated to create a void for a form of authoritarian dominance devoid of imagination (options) and humor (bonhommie). In this manner, whatever is sought as equality becomes sameness and mediocrity emerges by default. It is not surprising that the most creative work in landscape architecture today comes from places where authoritarian rules once dominated like China, Latin America, and Eastern Europe. In contrast, the work in western free societies (USA and Europe) has become predictable and dull while satisfying small constituencies of grievance, gender, and class. In a way, this "iron curtain" around the creative genius fosters periodic expressions of joy that by reason of their romanticism causes a rippling effect of amusement and goodness in the discipline and the culture as demonstrated by the Red Ribbon Park (Tanghe River) or the Sea Organ of Zadar in Croatia.

During the walk on the Camino de Santiago it was exciting to encounter local expressions of creative design rich in context and content as well as individuality like the Champollion Plaza in Figeac or the humor in León of a 6 foot high red garden pot holding a magnolia tree replicated in several locations to underline urban gardening or the Espolion promenade in Burgos on the banks of the Arlanzon River where the ghost of El Cid remains ever present. There were also the worn pathways though wheat fields and vineyards that had multiple authors in pilgrim steps across 10 centuries. The entire chain of spaces and places stood individually and collectively as singular jewels or strands to imbue the walk experience with a sense of singularity in diversity rather than sameness.

The liberation of imagination for the enrichment of culture and perception can only be brought about by an effort to achieve truth in vision and practice rather than the articulation of despair and catastrophe. If the profession of landscape architecture is a giver of hope to the world, there is a need to be less of a funeral director and more of a joyful triumphal chorus. Design in its best expression represents hope and possibility rather than entropy and malaise. For this reason it is important to liberate the academic studios on five fronts that will promote not only unfettered creativity but nourrish imagination:

1.- Integrity: Eliminate political correctness to promote honest and true dialogue with cordiality and respect. Remove the overbearing clouds of grievance and contrived perceptions of gender and race. Enable students to be humane in a climate of freedom and responsibility.

2.- Vocation: Select students by vocational measures rather than social-political quotas. Engage and accept the best candidates rather than the most apt to fulfill ideological frames. Focus on educating the best rather than indoctrinating the most. In the same manner, select faculty by capacity and capability to transfer knowledge and develop skills rather than empty credentials.

3.- Amplitude: Create a collective sense of engagement in a large mission and discipline rather than nurture the pursuit of small, safe, and insignificant projects. Expose students to the full dimension of the discipline and its challenges. Engage risk.

4.- Rationality: Emphasize rational analysis for design outcomes rather than emotion driven sentiments about people and environment. Love for the land or the earth needs to have solid basis for action rather than programmed or false measures of concern. There needs to be sentiment in the learning process but it does not need to be wrapped in empty sentimentality or erroneous suppositions.

5.- Truth: Embrace demonstrable truth in all engagements. Promote a critical spirit of evidence evaluation rather than dogmatic assent on all matters pertinent to design and its contextual expanse.

Perhaps the time has come to use the Cajun call: *Laissez les bontemps rouler*. Let the good times roll that the 21st century is calling true pilgrims to its assistance.

Walking Back from the Sunday Walk

Besides elation, a return from a walk invites some degree of conclusion or examination. On returning from France and Spain our backpack was full of things we had collected along the way and our mailbox had the delivery stubs for things we had sent that were no longer useful by matter or weight to our daily journey. Morever, some initial thoughts had grown weedlike into larger concepts after 66 days that merited either herbicide or cultivation. Not all thoughts are worth preserving although many can be blended or merged with other thoughts.

Creativity

Basilica of St. Isidore. León

R. Keith Sawyer. **Explaining Creativity: The Science of Human Innovation**. Oxford. 2006

Alexander Bain. **The Senses and the Intellect**. Nabu Press. 2011 (original 1855)

Thomas Lockwood, ed. **DesignThinking**. Allworth Press. 2010

Tim Brown. **Change by Design**. Harper. 2009

David B. Berman. **Do Good Design: How Designers Can Change the World**. New Riders. 2009

All along the route, there was the insistent call of a brief study on creativity that was done in response to an initiative for the "teaching" of creativity. Many sources were consulted and no definitive position was taken except to affirm the notion that true creativity was a gift (talent) that could be developed but never quite taught. This was not the required or accepted answer since the idea was to develop a class or a curriculum with potential for financial gain by the enrollment of students eager to be "creative". So, throughout the walk there was an undercurrent of search for the meaning of creativity and it surprisingly came at every turn in building and city form across various regions and periods. People without a psychology background rose by faith and commitment to learn trades and arts to the highest level of skill possible. Many learned the basics while a few went on to excel in remarkable fashion as head tradesmen or master builders. For every stonecutter in the marble quarries of Italy there was a possibility of inspired action by someone like Michelangelo or Donatello. Not all cutters became inspired sculptors or architects as much as not all wanted to be so. Many just wanted to learn a craft or a trade for daily life support while others aimed higher. In all, there were a few master builders that could guide a cathedral to completion but also many stone workers who could cut the right pieces to fit into a larger design etched by a master. There seemed to be joy in all by everyone. The light filtering through stained glass to bathe the curves of apses and columns spoke of a total craft effort. Hand drawings covered naves like wallpaper and images of saints and angels and biblical narrative floated about like special effects of a previous age. It was so with calligraphy as well as with mural painting. At the scriptorium (writing room) of the Teaching Abbey (Collegiale) of Saint Isidore in León my hands held the joyful evidence of both calligraphy and hymnody carefully copied in vellum by monks in the 12th century. The level of skill and love spoke loudly across time. No xerographic or laser color copy could match the exquisite lines and curves of calligraphy done as labor of worship in ink. Remarkably, the pages did not have the names of their authors in the lower right hand corner as is customary among my students. Yet, they spoke of personal and collective joy in craft. Each tradesman and crafstman was happy in fulfilling a calling as much as some superior artists and designers delighted in bringing to life a vision in stone or painting and sculpture of a higher meaning within and without the stone, the plaster or the canvas.

The notion of individualized creative options or conceptions of creativity (Keith Sawyer) was alien until the emergence of modern expressions of individuality under the influence of cognitive psychology (Alexander Bain). This parcelization of creativity as personal and individual has taken away from a larger view of craft as a community standard; however, it has been good for the self-esteem business and will prove to be a bonanza for the design business (innovation). Nevertheless; as demonstrated in ages past, the truly creative people will always surmount the easy definitions and ownership markings on the way to the production of truly superior work that has a community attribution and impact. The murals on the ceiling of the Sixtine Chapel were not just the expression of Michelangelo's genius, but also of a community that had nurtured and supported his endeavors. Rather than an isolated bright light, Michelangelo fed and was fed in the light of his community. Devising a new packaging for improved sales of breakfast cereals or packaging of beauty products might be considered "creative' (Thomas Lockwood) by advertising firms or academic business schools; but, it is far from the core of transcendent creative efforts like the invention of movable type or Michelangelo's work effort.

On more comprehensive terms, there is a notion that design as practiced by everybody answering to the apellation "designer" can have a transformative role. In this vein it is assumed that design alone can be used to solve the gravest problems on the face of the earth. This omnipotency of design and designers plays well with cause driven initiatives of various political purposes that somehow have an undercurrent of commerce and personal promotion. This notion is predominantly based on advertising and sees in packaging or re-invention of products or concepts a causal element that gives meaning and resolves conflicts like a soft drink slogan or the packaging of a new face moisturizer or the typography of a new music CD or t-shirt collection. Quite certainly, there is innovation in these efforts and some inherent level of creativity; however, the man that can carve out a rose from a turnip is not in the same creative dimension of someone who can conceive a system for recovery of a brownfield as a public space for the enjoyment of multitudes. The differentiation is truly important and must be kept in mind. The transformational power of design must be interpreted in context rather than pretext. Exhortations by some designers like Tim Brown and David Berman are well intentioned and can bear some fruit while the persuasive power of advertising to meet invented needs (ie: coke is it) calls for caution and sobermindedness. The drive-through ATM at my bank posts very prominent well designed signage in Braille that proclaims compliance with accessibility regulations (ADA) but there is no evidence that blind drivers are using the ATM or will do so in the near and urgent future. Yet, there is satisfaction in "helping" the handicapped navigate in the penumbra of daily life overcoming obstacles by human kindness attached to design product. Design in this way becomes merely an expression of competence in the manipulation of graphic elements and a heart tugging response to assigned sentiment.

A degree or course on or about creativity might offer fresh ways of looking (innovation) at common problems to proclaim "creative" solutions but it will not guide participants to truly creative work unless the element of risk is elevated to heroic levels that demand higher competence and longer commitment than a few hours at a computer screen. The reduction of design creativity to vain arguments about nomenclature free from vocational direction poses a problem that challenges truth upon which true design creativity acquires value. A PhD in physical science is not the same as a PhD in physics regardless of the administratrive imperative for equal quantification based solely on credentials rather than competence and capacity. Academia seems to be a fertil ground for what can be no more than nonsense (truculence) nurtured in some consensual manifest emotional destiny guided by equivocation and a desire to invent easily accessible ladders of success. True excellence and creativity go far beyond packaging and hype. Perhaps the second law of thermodynamics can take care of these notions.

The **Pont d'Artigues** on the headwaters of the Osse River near Condom

The **Pont Alexandre III** on the River Seine, Paris. Grand Palais can be seen in the background.

The importance of craft was also highlighted along the walk. Craft is an expression of creativity. Every night we consumed local products made by artisans in bread and cheese making as well as local culinary expressions. From duck to rabbit to sausage we sampled works of craft and passion along wih local wines and spirits that had earned a "domaine" (certification of origen) classification. There was a lot of pride in these products that imbued us with gratitude in response. In other areas from street pavement to cathedral quoins (cornerstones)and country stone walls it was evident that craftsmanship (responsibility) was present with pride bearing testimony to the dedication of people from past and present times. A Roman bridge still standing (Pont d'Artigues) between Condom and Larressingle has provided inspiration for similar bridges across the centuries. While there are new technologies and techniques for bridge building, the Roman arch bridge system still engages the imagination with its mathematical and geometric purity as well as its long life. In later years the fundamentals of Roman arc bridge building has supported variations in style (adornment) like the Alexander III bridge (a mixture of rococo and art nouveau) in Paris near the Grand Palais on the way from the Military Academy to the Champs Elysées. It is quite possible that in some journal or conference there can be an article or a presentation about new bridge technology that demeans the arc system and confines both the Pont d'Artigues and the Pont Alexandre III to the dustpile of engineering and art history. New advanced degrees would then be conferred and special awards issued. Yet, both bridges would still feed the imagination and carry people over the waters.

From reflective and people watching moments at the Plaza del Obradoiro next to the Cathedral in Santiago to an afternoon under the horsechestnuts at the Jardin des Tuileries, the dimension of the 66 day walk stands as a universal embrace that transforms beyond the distance and the steps. On the day of the Feast of Santiago (July 25) groups of demonstrators rallied next to the Cathedral for Galizia Nova (New Galicia) seeking more autonomy from the central government along with solutions to the abysmal poverty of the region. In this they were no different from the crowds that gathered almost 117 years earlier to witness the beheading of the French nobility by the Revolution at the Place de la Révolution (Place de la Concorde) just a few steps from Les Tuileries. Yet; in the evening, under the lights of a masterfully done graphic show projected on the facade of the Cathedral and under the eyes of the monarchy, the people rededicated the land to its patron saint

(St. James). The revolutionary ardor of the morning had dissipated into an act of faith and nationhood. The Galizia Nova movement will surely print more posters and handbills using all the creativity of graphic designers while Spain will continue to teeter on the verge of bankruptcy and illiterate shepherds will continue running cows and sheep along the correidoras. Pilgrims will also continue to walk to this place from all corners of Europe to hug St. James and earn a "compostella" executed in graceful calligraphy. The feet will be rested, no blisters left to attend and rich memories will feed connections to other events with bearing upon life and place. The pilgrimage really begins at the end of the walk.

Bibliography

The amount of works consulted is rather encyclopedic as well as multi-lingual. A vast amount of information was collected anecdotically. The following compilation reflects what can best be described as a synthesis of consulted works with bearing upon landscape architecture.

Andy Andrews. **How Do You Kill 11 Million People.** Thomas Nelson. 2011

Jay Appleton. **The Experience of Landscape**. John Wiley and Sons. 1996.

Donald Appleyard. **The View From The Road.** MIT Press. 1964

Gaston Bachelard. **The Poetics of Space.** Beacon Press. 1994

Alexander Bain. **The Senses and the Intellect**. Nabu Press. 2011 (original 1855)

Diana Balmori. **A Landscape Manifesto**. Yale. 2010

Roland Barthes. **Image, Music, Text**. Hill and Wang. New York. 1977

Simon Bell, Ingrid Sarlöv Herlin, Richard Stiles. **Exploring the Boundaries of Landscape Architecture.** Routledge. 2012

Anita Berrizbeitia. **Michael Van Valkenburgh Associates: Reconstructing Urban Landscapes**. Yale. 2009

Ed Casey. **The Fate of Place: A Philosophical History.** University of California Press.
1998

_____. **Representing Place: Landscape Painting and Maps**. University of Minnesota
Press. 2002

Michel Corajoud. Preamble/**The Landscape is the Place Where the Sky and the Earth Touch**
(Le Paysage c'est l'endroit ou le Ciel et la Terre se Touchent) Translation, Germán Cruz
Actes Sud/ENSP. Versailles.2010

James Corner. **Recovering Landscape: Essays in Contemporary Landscape Architecture**. Princeton Architectural Press. 1999. (288pp)

Michel de Certeau, **The Practice of Everyday Life.** University of California Press. Berkeley. 1984

Gilles Deleuze. **The Dice Throw**. In Margaret Iversen (ed). **Documents of Contemporary Art**. MIT Press. 2010.

Gareth Doherty and Mohsen Mostafavi. **Ecological Urbanism**. Lars Müller. 2010

Alice Foxley. **Distance and Engagement: Walking, Thinking and Making Landscape**. Vogt Landscape Architects. Lars Müller Publishers. Baden. 2010

Howard Gardner. **Truth, Beauty, and Goodness Reframed: Educating for the Virtues in the Twenty-First Century**. Basic Books. 2011

_____. **Frames of Mind: The Theory of Multiple Intelligences.** Basic Books. 1983

_____. **Intelligence Reframed: Multiple Intelligences for the 21st Century.** Basic Books. 2000

_____. **Multiple Intelligences: New Horizons in Theory and Practice.** Basic Books. 2006

Michael Gelb. **How to Think Like Leonardo da Vinci: Seven Steps to Genius Every Day**. Dell. 2000

James J. Gibson. **The Ecological Approach to Visual Perception**. Lawrence Erlbaum. 1986

Malcolm Gladwell. **Blink: The Power of Thinking Without Thinking.** Little, Brown, and Company. 2005

Fréderic Gros. **Marcher, Une Philosophie**. Flammarion. 2011 (new edition).

Edward T. Hall. **Beyond Culture.** Anchor. 1976.

_____. **The Hidden Dimension**. Anchor. 1990.

_____. **The Silent Language.** Anchor. 1973.

George Hargreaves. **Landscape Alchemy**. ORO Editions. 2009.

Charlotte Harris Rees. **Secret Maps of the Ancient World.** AuthorHouse. 2008

John Brickerhoff Jackson. **A Sense of Place, a Sense of Time**. Yale University Press. 1996.

Michel Jourdan, Jacques Vigne. **Marcher, Méditer**. Albin Michel. 1994/1998

Eric Kandel. **The Age of Insight: The Quest to Understand the Unconscious in Art, Mind, and Brain, from Vienna 1900 to the Present.** Random House. 2012

_____. **In Search of Memory: The Emergence of a New Science of Mind.** W W Norton. 2007

Christophe Lamoure. **Petit Philosophie du Marcheur.** Editions Milan. 2007

Susan Langer. **Feeling and Form**. Prentice Hall. 1977

Henri Lefebvre. **Rhythmanalysis: Space, Time and Every Day Life**. Continuum International Publishing Group. 2004

_____. **The Production of Space**. Blackwell Publishing Limited. 1991

Aldo Leopold. **The River of the Mother of God and Other Essays**. University of Wisconsin Press. 1992

Thomas Lockwood, ed. **DesignThinking**. Allworth Press. 2010

Alex MacClean. **Designs on the Land: Exploring America from the Air.** Thames and Hudson. 2003. With an introduction by James Corner.

Maurice Merleau-Ponty. **Phenomenology of Perception**. Routledge Classics. 2002

Joshua Meyrowitz. **No Sense of Place: The Impact of Electronic Media on Social Behavior.** Oxford University Press, USA. 1986

Rutherford H. Platt. **The Humane Metropolis: People and Nature in the 21st Century City**. University of Massachusetts Press. 2006

R. Keith Sawyer. **Explaining Creativity: The Science of Human Innovation**. Oxford. 2006

Simon Schama. **Landscape and Memory**. Vintage. 1996

Thomas Seely. **Honeybee Democracy.** Princeton.2010

Andy Stanley. **The Principle of the Path**. Thomas Nelson. 2011

Ken Smith. **Ken Smith: Landscape Architect**. The Monacelli Press. 2009

Anne Whiston Spirn. **The Language of Landscape.** Yale University Press. 2000

Marc Treib. Modern **Landscape Architecture: A Critical Review.** MIT Press. 1993

_____. **Spatial Recall: Memory in Architecture and Landscape**. Routledge. 2009

_____. **Meaning in Landscape Architecture and Gardens**. Routledge. 2011

_____. **The Content of Landscape Form (The Limits of Formalism).** Landscape Journal. 20:2001. p119-140

Yi-Fun Tuan. **Space and Place: The Perspective of Experience**. University of Minnesota Press. 2001

_____. **Topophilia: A Study of Environmental Perceptions, Attitudes, and Values.** Columbia University Press. 1990

Henry David Thoreau. **Walden**. Digireads.com. 2005

_____. **On Walking**. Atlantic Monthly. 1862. (Lecture given at Concord Lyceum on April 23, 1851, published posthumously)

Paul Virilio. **Negative Horizon: An Essay in Dromoscopy.** Continuum. London. 2005

_____. **A Landscape of Events**. MIT Press. Cambridge. 2000

_____. **Lost Dimension**. Semiotext(e). New York. 1991

_____. *War and Cinema: The Logistics of Perception.* Verso. London. 1989

_____. *Speed and Politics: An Essay on Dromology.* Semiotext(e). New York. 1977/1986

Charles Waldheim. **The Landscape Urbanism Reader.** Princeton. 2006

Wim Wenders. **A Sense of Place**. Verlag Der Autoren. 2005

Edward O. Wilson. **Sociobiology: The New Synthesis.** Belknap Press. 1975/2000

_____. **The Social Conquest of Earth**. Liveright/W. W. Norton and Company. 2012

_____. **Biophilia**. Harvard. 1984

_____. **On Human Nature**. Harvard. 1978/2004

_____. **Consilience: The Unity of Knowledge.** Vintage. 1999

_____. **The Ants.** Harvard, 1990

James E. Zull. **The Art of Changing the Brain: Enriching the Practice of Teaching by Exploring the Biology of Learning**. Stylus. 2002. page 117

Guidebooks and Websites

Docteur Jean Boyer. **Saint Jacques de Compostelle: Légendes et Chemins d'Hier et d'Aujourd'hui.** Editions l'Etoile du Sud. 1999

John Brierly. **Camino de Santiago.** Camino Guides/Findhorn Press. 2009

Marie-Virginie Cambriels and Jacques Cloteau. **Miam Miam Dodo: Le Chemin de Saint Jacques de Compostelle: El Camino Francés**. Les Editions du Vieux Crayon. 2009

Christian Champion. **Le Chemin de Compostelle: Voie du Puiy en Velay.** Chemin du Pèlerin. 2010

Lauriane Cloteau and Jacques Cloteau. **Miam Miam Dodo: Le Chemin de Saint Jacques de Compostelle: La Voie du Puy**. Les Editions du Vieux Crayon. 2008

Dana Facaros and Michael Pauls. **Northern Spain.** Cadogan Guides/The Globe Pequot Press. 2006

Dorling Kindersley Publishing. **Spain**. Eyewitness Travel Guide. 2001

David M. Gitlitz and Linda Kay Davidson. **The Pilgrimage Road to Santiago: The Complete Cultural Handbook**. St. Martin's Griffin. 2000

Jean-Yves Grégoire. **Guide du Camino Francès.** Rando Editions. 2010

Everest. **Mapa Turístico del Camino de Santiago**. Editorial Everest. León

Andy Symington. **Footprint Handbooks: Northern Spain**. Footprint Books/Publishers Group West. 2003

Michelin. **Spain.** Green Guide. Michelin et Cie. 2006

Paco Nadal. **El Camino de Santiago a Pie.** El Pais/Aguilar. 1999/2006

Cordula Rabe. **Camino de Santiago: De los Pinineos a Santiago de Compostela**. Rother Guía Excursionista. Munich. 2007

Alison Raju. **The Way of St. James: Le Puy to the Pyrinees. A Walker's Guide**. Cicerone. 2006

Alison Raju. **The Way of St. James: Pyrinees - Santiago - Finisterre. A Walker's Guide**. Cicerone. 2003

TopoGuide GR65: **sentier vers Saint-Jacques-de-Compostelle, via Le Puy > Le Puy - Figeac**. Fédération Française de la Randonnée Pédestre. Paris. 2006

TopoGuide GR65: **sentier vers Saint-Jacques-de-Compostelle, via Le Puy > Figeac - Moissac**. Fédération Française de la Randonnée Pédestre. Paris. 2006

TopoGuide GR65: **sentier vers Saint-Jacques-de-Compostelle, via Le Puy > Moissac - Roncevaux**.Fédération Française de la Randonnée Pédestre. Paris. 2007

Chemin de St. Jacques de Compostelle (http://compostellane. over-blog.com)

Camino Santiago Información (http://infocamino.com)

Albergues/Guía del Camino de Santiago (http://caminodesantiago. consumer.es/albergues/

Backpack 45 (http://www.backpack45.com/camino2p2.html)

The Confraternity of St. James (http://www.csj.org.uk/)

Godesalco (http://www.godesalco.com)

Mundicamino (http://www.mundicamino.com)

Hébergements sur le Chemin de Compostelle (http://www. chemindecompostelle.com)

Compostela or Certificate of Completion of pilgrimage walk is confered upon confirmation of at least 10 consecutive days of walkin on the Camino. It is given by the Office of the Cathedral of Saint James in Santiago de Compostela. The shortest distance is from León. 2010 was a Holy Year (Annus Sancti) because the Feast of St. James fell on a Sunday.

The Chapter of this Holy Apostolic Metropolitan Cathedral of Santiago, custodian of the Seal of Saint James' Altar, to all faithful and pilgrims who come from everywhere over the world as an act of devotion, under vow or promise to the Apostle's Tomb, our Patron and Protector of Spain, witnesses in the sight of all who read this document, that:

German Cruz

has visited devoutly this Sacred Church in a religious sense (pietatis causa).

Witness where of I hand this document over to him/her, authenticated by the seal of this Sacred Church.
Given in Santiago de Compostela on the 23 rd day of July
A.D. 2010 (Holy Year)

(Signed) Canonic Deputy for Pilgrims"

Credential or Passport of the Pilgrim. Issued by a church at the beginning of the walk. It is stamped every night by the refuge or place of rest. Each one has a distinctive style and bear witness to the journey. Usually given in the morning before departure.

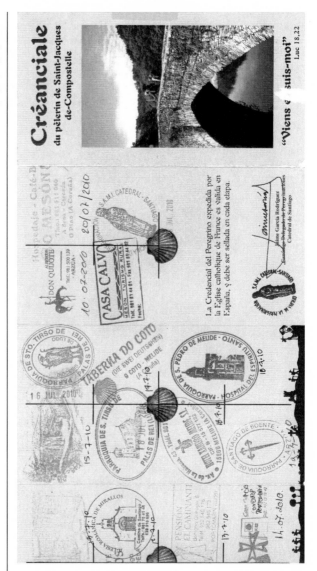

Part Two

Walk
and
Place

Sixty Six Days
and One Thousand Miles
Under the Milky Way
in the Via Podensis
and the Camino Francés

4.5 MILLION STEPS

Just about 32 hours before boarding Air France to Paris. The flight might take over 1 hour longer in order to avoid the ash cloud from the recent volcano eruption. Hope the delay is not so long that it may imperil the connection to the High Speed train at 12:30 at Gare de Lyon. There is another train later in the afternoon. Just eager to get to Le Puy and start the walk asap. Finished doing final packing of the backpack. Some things will not make the trip. Surprising how little one needs when choices are narrow and light.

Pondered about distance and figured out that at 3 steps per meter it would take 4.5 million steps to reach Santiago de Compostela. Sounds like a really big undertaking but it becomes comfortable in the awareness that it is a sum total over 66 days rather than a one day event. Still it is an awesome number. Kind of similar to the number of stars that will march with us above in the Milky Way (give or take a few).

Wonderful wedding yesterday. Perhaps magnificent is a better adjective. Great reception afterwards with friends who traveled many miles to share in the moment. Sometimes the heart expands greatly to hold these sublime moments of joy and blessing. Robert looked happy and manly. Liesl was a dream of young womanhood. Wonderfully fit couple. May they share a lifelong gift of joy in love.

Will talk again from Le Puy at the feet of the Massif Central in Haute Loire.

ANXIETY

Just about 72 hours to go before our departure for France and than another 48 hours before the walk begins in earnest. There is anticipation in the air. Some might call it anxiety. It might well be a combination plate adorned by a great desire of just getting it done. On the whole, getting there just amounts to getting the beginning done.

Essentially, the bags are packed along with expectations and a few euros to help the economies. For a while we thought of ourselves as a new Marshall Plan but we are content to being just the Cruz Happy Plan and Good Will March. Of course, there are Euros involved but the main ingredients are really the heart and the mind.

St. Paul spoke of "being anxious for nothing" which was easy for him to say while in chains under Roman guard. Ha . . . ha . . ha. My anxiety is merely based on the many gates we have to cross and the monstruous bureaucracy tending them. Travelling with a backpack full of things wrapped in compression plastic bags should cause some pause in the system at the least auspicious moment. Perhaps like St. Paul I might have the grace to smile and put up with it. Just thought that the system would be vastly different if travellers in Air Force One had to endure it.

In any event, we are ready for take-off on Monday at 5 PM or so. However, there is a wedding before that that is kind of important. Robert and Liesl will exchange vows on Saturday afternoon. Big step for the little boy I once held in wonder at 9 lbs plus in Tampa Women's Hospital. Much water has past under the bridge. Good water with wonderful currents of memories.

A REGION TO START

The Auvergne department (state) waits for us in SE France. It is one of the least populated regions of France with an alpine volcanic landscape full of meadows and gorges, Lots of geese (foie gros), game, farms, goats, and meadows.

In the SE corner of Auvergne is Haute Loire, The high region where the Loire River begins its flow to the Atlantic. Its capital is Le Puy en Velay from where we will begin our walk. The name Auvergne comes from the Gallic tribe of the Arvenii whose leader Vercingetorix was defeated and captured by Julius Caesar who included the region in the conquered lands of southern France which he called Aquitaine. Vercingetorix became a symbol of Gallic rebellion and pride even to the present time. The comic strip "Asterix" keeps the feeling alive today. Over time, the Auvergne has been possessed by various kings and royal houses after the Romans ceded it to the Visigoths in 475. By the 12th century Aquitane had become a possession of the English king Henry II upon his marriage to Eleanor (Duchess) of Aquitaine. Eleanor has been described as "beautiful and just, imposing and modest, humble and elegant" and "a queen that surpassed all the queens of the world". Before her marriage to Henry II, Eleanor had been consort of Louis VII of France and as Queen of France exerted considerable power since her lands exceeded the territory of the French kingdom. She participated in the 2nd Crusade (1147-49) to protect Jerusalem from the Turks and had her marriage annulled in 1152 due to Louis's jealousy and probably physical abuse. She bore no male heirs to the French throne but gave Henry 5 sons and 3 daughters that served to expand the Plantagenet family imprint upon medieval Europe. Her sons: William, who died at the age of 3, Henry, Richard the Lion Heart, Geoffrey, duke of Brittany, and John (Lackland) who inherited the crown of England

in 1199. Her daughters married kings in Saxony, Castile, and Sicily. Someone suggested that by sheer production of rulers and royalty Eleanor de Aquitaine was the "grandmother of Europe". Semi-imprisoned in England for 16 years after the failure of her sons rebellion against their father. Eleanor emerged in 1189 after the death of Henry II with more energy and power. She administered the realm while Richard the Lion-Heart went on a Crusade, ransomed him from the Duke of Austria, sustained the Plantagenet domination and insured peace with the emerging Capetian kings of France. After her death in 1204 at the monastery of Fontevrault in Anjou, her lands (Aquitaine) remained loyal to England while Normandy fell to the French. So we will walk on a rugged land quite similar to the character of her ancestral mistress.

After Eleanor, the lands of Aquitaine passed on through various names and regimes to the French Crown to eventually become several modern departments in the late 18th century.

So much for the history lesson. It is good to know that places we do not really know have left an imprint on land and people. We will be paying close attention to this aspect as we shuffle on to Santiago. Karen got a camera for Mother's day and has already become a fanatic photo shooter. Eventually, she will turn out to be good photographer. The excitement builds up and now the days pulsate with anticipation. Everything is ready. One week from today we will be en route to Paris

ITINERARY

This was the intended itinerary which was subsequently modified as our feet (and bodies) engaged the land. The walking pace was initially and hopefully estimated at 4 km/hr depending on topography, weather and physical conditioning plus amenities found on the road that merit engagement and exploration. For the most part we tried to hit the road around 7:30 AM (that's 6 hours earlier than EDST) and expected to arrive at our destination around 3PM. Some of the longer stages called for an earlier departure. A few long daily journeys responded to availability of accommodations as much as walking ambition. Miles are rounded up.

May 17: Air: Chicago-Paris
May 18: Train: Paris—St. Etienne—Le Puy (Combination of High Speed and regional narrow gauge rail)
May 19: REST/Trip Organization in Le Puy (See the town, get last minute supplies, get credential)
May 20: Le Puy - Montbonnet: 16 km (10 miles)
May 21: Montbonnet—Monistrol d'Allier: 14.5 km (9 miles)
May 22: Monistrol d'Allier—Falzet: 23 km (14 miles)
May 23: Falzet—Le Rouget: 21.3 km (13 miles)
May 24: Le Rouget—Aumont-Aubrac: 18 km (11 miles)
May 25: Aumont-Aubrac—Montgros: 23.5 km (15 miles)
May 26: Montgros—St, Chely d'Aubrac: 20 km (13 miles)
May 27: St. Chely d'Aubrac—Espalion: 22 km (14 miles)
May 28: Espalion—Massip: 25 km (16 miles(
May 29: Massip—Conques: 21 km (13 miles)
May 30: Conques—Decazeville: 19 km (12 miles)
May 31: Decazeville—Figeac: 28.5 km (18 miles)

June 1: Figeac—Grealou: 20.5 km (13 miles)
June 2: Grealou—Limogne sur Quercy: 28 km (18 miles)
June 3: Limogne—Lalbenque: 21.3 km (13 miles)
June 4: Lalbenque—Lascabanes: 24 km (15 miles)
June 5: Lascabanes—Lauzerte: 22 km (14 miles)
June 6: Lauzerte—Moissac: 24.5 km (15 miles)
June 7: Moissac—Auvillar: 20,5 km (13 miles)
June 8: Auvillar—Castet-Arrouy: 22.3 km (14 miles)
June 9: Castet—Castelnou sur l'Avignon: 29 km (18 miles)
June 10: Caltelnou—Montreal du Gers: 27,8 km (17 miles)
June 11: Montreal du Gers—Eauze; 16.5km (10 miles)
June 12: REST in Eauze
June 13: Eauze—Nogaro: 20 km (12 miles)
June 14: Nogaro—Aire sur l'' Adour: 28.2 km (17 miles)
June 15: Aire sur l'Adour: Miramont: 18.2 km (11 miles)
June 16: Miramont—Chateau Meracq: 24.5 km (15 miles)
June 17: Chateau Meracq—Arthez: 27.5 km (17 miles)
June 18: Arthez de Bearn—Sauvelade: 18 km (11 miles)
June 19: Sauvelade—Lichos: 26.8 km (16 miles)
June 20: Lichos—Gaineko Etxea: 26.8 km (16 miles)
June 21: Gaineko: St. Jean Pied de Port: 21.4 km (13 miles)
June 22: REST in St. Jean Pied de Port (at the feet of the Pyrenees)
June 23: St Jean—Roncesvalles: 25 km (15 miles)
Enter Spain
June 24: Roncesvalles—Zubiri: 21.8 km (13 miles)

June 25: Zubiri—Pamplona: 23.6 km (14 miles)

June 26: Pamplona—Puente la Reina: 24 km (15 miles)

June 27: Puente La Reina: Estella: 21.7 km (13 miles)

June 28: Estella/Lizarra—Los Arcos: 21.3 km (13 miles)

June 29: Los Arcos—Logroño: 27.9 km (17 miles)

June 30: Logroño—Najera: 29.9 km (23 miles)

July 1: Najera—S. Domingo: 21 km (13 miles)

July 2: S. Domingo—Belorado: 25.3 km (15 miles)

July 3: Belorado—Agés: 27.7 km (17 miles)

July 4: Agés—Burgos: 25.6 km (16 miles)

July 5: REST in Burgos (Home of El Cid)

July 6: Burgos—Hontanas: 29,5 km (18 miles)

July 7: Hontanas—Itero de la Vega: 20.8 km (12 miles)

July 8: Itero—Carrión de los Condes: 33.3 km (21 miles)

July 9: Carrión—Terradillos: 26.7 km (16 mi)

July 10: Terradillos—El Burgo: 32.2 km (20 miles)

July 11: El Burgo Ranero—Villarete: 25.2 km (16 miles)

July 12: Puente de Villarete—León: 12.3 km (8 miles)

July 13: León—Villadangos del Páramo: 28.6 km (18 miles)

July 14: Villadangos—Astorga: 29.1 km (19 miles)

July 15: Astorga—Rabanal del Camino: 20,9 km (12 miles)

July 16: Rabanal—Molinaseca: 24.7 km (15 miles)

July 17: Molinaseca—Cacabelos: 23.3 km (14 miles)

July 18: Cacabelos—Ruitelán: 27.8 km (17 miles)

July 19: Ruitelán—Ponfría: 22.1 km (14 miles)

July 20: Ponfría—Sarria: 27.2 km (17 miles)

July 21: Sarria—Portomarín: 21.9 km (13 miles)

July 22: Portomarín—Palas del Rei: 26.8 km (16 miles)

July 23: Palas del Rei—Arzúa: 29.5 km (19 miles)

July 24: Arzúa—Lavacolla: 30 km (19 miles)

July 25: Lavacolla—Santiago: 11.2 km (7 miles) Get credential stamped
Celebration at Plaza del Obradoiro

July 26: Santiago

July 27: Santiago - Paris (RENFE to Hendaye/TGV to Paris)

July 28: Paris (Tour)

July 29: Paris (Versailles)

July 30: Paris (Musee Rodin/Tuileries/Bookstores)

July 31: Paris (Jardin de Luxembourg)

August 1: Paris—Chicago—Indianapolis - Muncie

WALKING IN HISTORY

In the Middle Ages, a network of foot paths carried pilgrims to the shrine at Santiago from every country. The roads went over the Pyrenees and into Spain, either by way of the great monastery at Roncesvalles, or via that of SantaCristina and the Somport Pass. These main routes became "The Camino Francés". A 778 km walk to Santiago in western Galicia. The portion from Le Puy to Roncesvalles is the "Via Podensis" or "Path of Power" (approximately 720 km) that collected pilgrims from Switzerland and points in Germany, Austria, Poland, the Czech Republic, and Slovakia. In contemporaryFrance the Le Puy route follows and is often integrated with the GR 65, a portion of the Grande Randonée (The Great Hike), a system of walking and hikingtrails all across France with refuges (gîtes), hostels, and services all along the route in villages and farmsteads.

Santiago despite its far away location, exerted an inordinate appeal to travelers from pre-Christian times. It lay enveloped in the mists of the Cantabric Sea with Celtic images and landscapes of menhirs and faded gods calling to the imagination and courage of people and tribes. The route to Santiago was a Roman trade-route. It was nicknamed by travellers "la voie ladee" (the Milky Way) for the expanse of stars above its route that seemed to point toward the edge of the known world (Cape Finisterre). The mysteries of earth and sky seemed to come together at Santiago. Thus, The Way of Saint James or El Camino has been that road under the stars that guided adventurers and pilgrims far away from home to a place both mysterious and almost unreachable that conferred peace, joy and satisfaction to its walkers.

The vast majority of those who walk The Way of Saint James today, are not experienced walkers at all nor pilgrims in search of redemption. Most are just short and long distance hikers seeking the solace of the way and the opportunity to enjoy nature and landscape. The road is special by design. Most long-distance footpaths avoid not only large towns but even quite small villages as well; the Way of Saint James, on the other hand, because of its historic origins and the need for shelter, deliberately seeks them out. It passes through ancient places rich in art and architectural masterpieces as well as long expanses of cultivated fields and primeval forests. The foundation of France as well as the armature of Spain are evident in each step.

As Karen and I get closer to take up this walk, our imagination begins to race with images and possibilities. The expectation is huge as well as the anxiety. Our spreadsheet is well set to guide us to shelters and places with contact numbers and distances. However, it does not tell us much about the mind and the heart. We will soon find the way out of our current sense of overwhelming movement into some unknown dimension. This is truly a very big enterprise despite the conveniences and knowledge that will surround us. While it is not the same as Columbus crossing the Atlantic, it is just the same as a leap into the sky seeking to land on a cloud. This experience is apt to expand our minds and hearts to sizes never quite expected before. Each walker on the way is like every walker before yet unlike any other walker. The legacy of the experience of body, soul, and spirit can be recorded in a narrative with scholarly underpinnings or in soft memories of place and being. Perhaps both will come about. There is only expectation and the will to receive that which is expected and yet unknown.

We also carry your expectations and the need to connect you to this experience. By means of this blog we expect to share a great deal and then share more in writings and drawings that will be shared at a later date. Unlike medieval pilgrims we have technology on our side while trying hard to keep it from interfering in the joy of seeing, hearing, touching and smelling and sensing the places and the people. Perhaps a bit of tasting will also come into place through wine and cuisine.

Itinerary shown in the previous pages will enable you to judge distances and places and the map in the following page will serve to place our walk in context with the lands we will be crossing.

THE CAMINOS IN EUROPE

Map (also shown in page 15) shows the extensive network of routes that connected all of Europe with Santiago de Compostela. Some or most of these routes are now parallel or near national roads and have become walkways and linear greenways under national or regional systems.

Our walk (red line) will go from Le Puy to Roncesvalles on the border with Spain and then

Weather in Le Puy is now (May 5th) a bit rainy with temperatures between upper 40s and mid 60s pretty much like hereabouts. However, very soon things will get drier and warmer (mid 60s to upper 70s). Spain will be hot like August in Indiana (80s to 90s).

In all, the French section will be pleasant with many bakeries along the route. Spain is another thing but by then we will be sprite, buffed, and well toughened after more than one month on

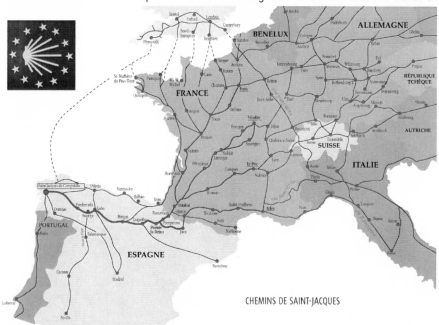

CHEMINS DE SAINT-JACQUES

flow (by then a decided and strong march) to Pamplona, Sahagun, Leon, Ponferrada and Santiago. We will leave Le Puy on May 20th and arrive in Santiago on the morning of July 25th around 11AM to witness the great jubilee celebration of the Feast of Saint James. We will cross Roncesvalles (Roncevaux) around June 22nd.

A "puy" is a volcanic stele (column) or "mountain" typical of the Auverge region. These "steles" were formed in prehistoric times and now host castles or churches or monuments.

the march. It is all quite exciting and appears so simple.

The days are getting quite exciting and it is time to load up the backpacks and get a feel for their weight and for all the stuff we might not need. Our desire for comfort makes us carry more than enough of all things in the fear that we will need them and they might not be available in the European versions of our drugstores and foodstores. Yet, how do they manage to live as well as us? It might take a few "packing" sessions to get the hang (hahahaha) of it.

We will leave for Chicago on May 12th to have dinner with the in-laws and get the wedding events off to a great start. Our resident student and some friends will take care of Casa de Cruz and Mimi the cat. Our student resident will come in a couple of weeks for the rest of the Summer. This is truly a complex adventure. Amidst all the trepidation we welcome the challenge and look forward to exciting events and wonderful surprises. We will try to post often in as much as the wi-fi communication network allows my Blackberry to connect. We will also send post cards as we can. Our walking times might not always coincide with the Post Office times of operation.

FIRST DAY

Walk of 16 km between Le Puy and Montbonnet. Very steep exit from Le Puy with a curving road hiding its slopes. Hard to figure out distance. Road has been hit by heavy Spring rains that have managed to pull out tons of rocks (4 to 6 inches) that make walking treacherous and hard on speed. Took us about one hour and a half to do 5 km. The next portion took us for about 4 miles along the edge of a canyon carved out by the Doliason River. The path was a narrow foot wide rut with large and small stones as well as water running from the fields. Nothing could be harder. I managed to lose my balance and have my first mud bath. After two hours we covered the 3.5 km to St. Christophe somehow beaten by the road, the rocks, the hills. Over a cheese sandwich (croque monsieur) with Orangina we decided to cover the last 8 km by taxi to a very nice refuge. Nice beds in a dormitory and a very excellent meal have renewed our spirits. More importantly, our backpacks will be taken to our next destination to enable us to get our legs in tune with road and its conditions.

There were about 50 pilgrims with us on the road. Our refuge is hosting 18 tonight. The weather is cool and windy (upper 40s). The sun is trying to be of help but it hides in the clouds.

We march on across the edge of the Massif Central in beautiful land with fields of winter wheat, clover, and recently plowed earth.

Views of Le Puy en Velay

PROFILES

These general profiles of the Via Podensis (Le Puy Route/Chemin de Puy) produced by www.godesalco.com (Arturo J. Murias) show the varied topography of the terrain with location of main cities and pilgrim hostals. The help provided by this type of map is invaluable in developing a better understanding of conditions and defining plans for walking and staging. Seen in profile, the route acquires a larger dimension that somehow justifies the impact of the ground upon the body and mind of the pilgrims.

The enemy is not so much the weather but the topography and its incidental rock, mud, and

marcheurs) distracted by flowers, farmsteds, textures and smells. It is rather incredible to think that for centuries other people have trod this road or whatever passes for it. Our shoes are designed for trekking in wet ground and we wear wool socks that repel water. Imagine a 10th century pilgrims wearing sandals and probably no socks. Was their pace faster? Did they stop to look at landscape?

How many set their feet exactly were we set ours? How far did they walk each day? The distance between convents and old hostals was greater then. It seems like we do not walk alone. The steps collected over centuries march with us and the land bears witness along with birds, cows, sheep, and houses. There is no silence. The trail

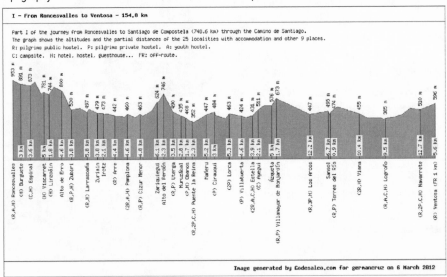

manure components. Late Spring at this altitude is rather wet with cold sunlight. Surely, as the journey advances and the season moves into Summer we will be wishing for cold days and nights before a fireplace and a bowl of bean soup. Cows and sheep dominate the meadows and the roads. In places the trail has fallen victim to fresh and constant hoof action that makes feet twist and turn in the mud. Still, some pilgrims walk in Olympic fashion moving fast and determined like the rabbit in Alice. We are the slow pokes (douce

speaks constantly. In future years, others might search for our traces and voices. Others might step right where we stepped today. The earth accepts all and keeps all.

Of course; like horizontal maps, the vertical profiles also present an exaggerated view of the land. Both views serve only to represent a condition that can only be truly measured by experience As we will discover, the steepness

might be real but it is our hearts that determine
its real impact.

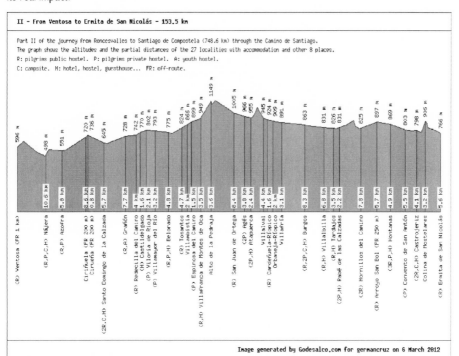

Part IV of the journey from Roncesvalles to Santiago de Compostela (748.6 km) through the Camino de Santiago.
The graph shows the altitudes and the partial distances of the 32 localities with accommodation and other 10 places.
R: pilgrims public hostel. P: pilgrims private hostel. A: youth hostel.
C: campsite. H: hotel, hostel, guesthouse... FR: off-route.

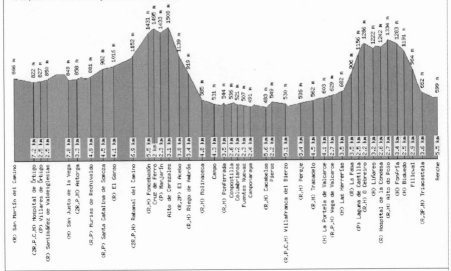

V - From Renche to Santiago de Compostela - 133.7 km

Part V of the journey from Roncesvalles to Santiago de Compostela (748.6 km) through the Camino de Santiago.
The graph shows the altitudes and the partial distances of the 22 localities with accommodation and other 5 places.
R: pilgrims public hostel. P: pilgrims private hostel. A: youth hostel.
C: campsite. H: hotel, hostel, guesthouse... FR: off-route.

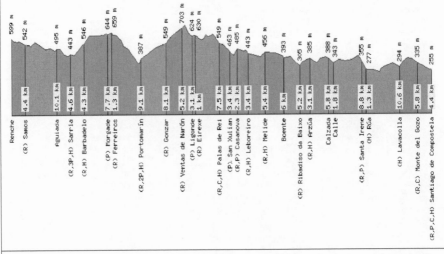

MONISTROL D'ALLIER

Leaving Le Puy yesterday at 2062 ft one climbs to 3656 ft at Montbonnet for an overnight rest from where we headed today under cloudy skies to Saint Privat d'Allier at 2937 ft, then to Rochegude at 3101 ft to eventually reach Monistrol d'Allier at 2042 ft. It was a rollercoaster that tested our legs as well as our determination. The Allier river runs SE to NE across the land from the Massif Central to the left bank of the Loire. One marches up and down on the slopes of the canyons that contain its drainage system ever aware of the Allier running fresh alpine water several hundred feet below. Despite the topographic challenge we enjoyed a cool Spring morning in the mid 40s walking often on soft wet soil from the rain in the previous day and night. Some sheep in a nearby meadow seemed quite comfortable under their wool while looking at us with curious eyes. These black sheep of Velay have been in this region from the times of the Celtic invasion in the 3rd and 4th centuries BC. Their cheese is pleasantly soft with a hard shell. After about 2 miles we hit a paved road that takes us after another 2 miles to the small village of Le Chier where a farmsted made up of a cluster of homes from various periods frame a commons that holds a long trough. It looked as if several generations had progressively occupied the houses bringing about changes fitted to new lifestyles. The houses resembled classic Roman homes built initially from cut rock and lately with CMUs and other modern materials. We sat at a picnic table in front of city hall surrounded by cows while enjoying a sheepsmilk cheese sandwich with an orange drink that gave us enough energy to keep on walking to Saint Privat. The pilgrimage road used to go northward from Montbonnet to La Chaise-Dieu (from Latin casa dei = House of God), in reference to the Benedictine abbey which was founded in 1043. Eventually, the route was changed to follow an old Roman road that shortened the walk to Saint Privat and avoided some inhospitable areas. The abbey at Chaise-Dieu had over 300 monks and 42 outlying priories (convents) among which was the one at Saint Privat. The abbey at Chaise-Dieu continued to grow throughout the Middle Ages, becoming the motherhouse of further congregations of Black Monks (Benedictines wear black habits or cassocks). Pope Clement VI began his vocation as a monk at Chaise- Dieu and was the patron of the vast abbey church (built 1344-1350) that became a suitable setting for his tomb. The monks were driven out and the abbey secularized during the French Revolution. From Saint Privat a stone paved road leads to Rochegude where a chapel and a fresh water creek welcome the walkers before plunging into a downward pathway over rock to Pratclaux. Over time, the path has been eroded by natural and human forces that make the walk quite challenging where some sections have a slope greater than 20% while others have deep ruts or very slippery surface. We made the one-mile descent in about 2 hours rather than a normal 30 minutes for the distance. All the way we were filled with fear of falling down and breaking some bones. It was a truly scary section. We decided then to skip the next day walk over a similar terrain and take a taxi to Sauges. Several fellow walkers did the same thing. Land on a map is quite different from land under your feet.

SAUGES

The days have moved quite fast despite the reluctance of our legs. From the Villarette d'Apchier on Sunday to the Medieval preserve of Sauges some 100 km apart today. It is a move caused by the impossibility of doing 20 km marches every day and still take good looks all around. The initial rate of 4 km per hour is more of a competition pace that is centered on getting from point to point while we are more concerned with finding and connecting dots very much like sailors reading the skies with an astrolabe. "Villaret" is kind of the French way of suburban expansion with touches of Plan Unit Development, New Urbanism, and some administrative capacity. These are small neighborhoods with very functional housing that fits the general character of the land and the community (according to local leader).Sunday night at dinner time we had several "education professionals" at the table and conversation bounced on issues of pedagogy and creativity. There was no agreement as to teaching methodology but much to my surprise it was agreed that creativity was a gift and could not be taught. The discussion could have gone longer had it not being by the arrival of the cheese tray that just before dessert and coffee marks the end of a French meal. There was a very spirited discussion about particular qualities of each cheese along with wowing and lip smacking when sampling various goat and cow milk cheeses manufactured by artisans near and far. My cheese passion is not as pronounced as that of my French table mates but it is somewhat impressive that people become passionate about craftsmanship of any sort.From the Villarette we walked to a spot on the road where a rebuilt chapel stands. It was the anchor of a hospital (both medical and hosting type) that welcomed pilgrims on previous centuries. Various conflicts of religion and politics had brought the facility to ruins but early in the 20th century the chapel was rebuilt from original drawings just 300 feet away from a miraculous spring that refreshed and cured pilgrims (walkers) since the 12th century. All is wrapped around the life and deeds of St. Roch (Roque or Rocco in Spanish or Italian). In a rather hot day at the end of a 12 km walk, the water from the fountain renewed us and the shade from the chapel cooled us while waiting for a ride to our bed and breakfast for the night.A wnderful and quite dynamic 76 year old widow hosted us in Ste. Eulalie with coq au vin, great salad and many delicious home made all things of which she was quite proud. She collects raspberries in the nearby woods and makes awesome syrup to flavor water and other drinks. The talk of cheese craftmanship from the night before was reaffirmed with her presentation of cheese creations of her own. In this rather isolated and self-sufficient farm country there is a lot of pride in personal achievement along with strong faith. Not just of the going to church on holiday kind but of a belief in transcendacy and connection. We decided to push the calendar and travelled across the region known as the Aubrac (the outback) that is kind of gently ondulating and dedicated to cattle grazing. It produced grass fed beef of superior quality and creamy milk that is transformed into great butters and cheeses (do not ask for oliomargarine around these parts or 1% milk). It was a delightful 100 km drive across many farm roads and towns aboard the van that transports backsacks from refuge to refuge. Kind of a FedEx for backpackers that has grown into a thriving business in the past 10 years. The driver goes like a man possessed between 8 and 12 hitting refuges along the Way of St. James while others do other routes. The narrow streets and alleys along with narrow farm and mountain roads provide a test of skill to the driver and most certainly strengthens the prayer life of the passengers. But there are wonderful vistas and places coming at you on 5 speed manual transmission. A number of obstacles hit the route like a herd of cows adorned with flower crowns and French flags that take over the road on their parade from the high grazing lands to the lower areas where fescue and other good milk producing grasses are tender and fresh. It is calving season also and Karen has fallen in love with many crazy, big eyed calves. She talks to them but they only speak a bovine dialect of French.We are in Sauges for a two day immersive experience in the Middle Ages. Our future itinerary will consist of 10 to 12 km marches with lots of sightseeing and note taking. We had not planned an Olympic event. Food has been great but we are going to one meal a day with a fruit snack in the evening for the sake of leaving some part of us in French and Spanish soil.Conversation is great with people we encounter several times either walking or relaxing. Some gave us a "medal of courage" for our "descent" from Rochegude to Montbonnet on our second stage.May all be well with all. We carry a constellation of friends in mind and heart.

SAUGES (Part Two)

Found some English hikers in this medieval outpost and had a lot of laughs recalling Monty Python and the Holy Grail stories. Seriously; however, this town is quite beholden to its past and its authenticity. Specially after lugging our backpacks up a 3 story winding staircase and opening our windows at four stories above the slate roofs below us and watching the cliffs of the rocky elevations across the way. Really expected Eric Idle and the Python gang to march on the plaza below. Everything is medieval here except the prices and the food. I had a dream of Muncie becoming a museum of the second industrial age complete with striking workers, forced production runs, bed and breakfast services, cozy bars with gambling machines, sidewalk cafes, bookstores, interactive museums, sanctuaries, houses of worship, cooperating university, generous civic minded faculty, and other assorted graces that would attract visitors and employ many people. Then I woke up. Truly like Lope de Vega affirmed: "life is a dream and dreams are just dreams" On our path there have been many remnants and memories of a distant past and we have come to believe again in tradition and historic context. We have been walking pathways in woods where Templar Knights stood on guard to protect pilgrims (did they have sirens on their mounts?),seen chapels and churches that have stood wars and "programs" of state and religion, touched and drank the clear waters of rivers and fountains that have refreshed the soreness and thirsts of generations, sat and thought about land and time from Celtic to Germanic tribes to Roman camps, bridges, and roads, marvelled at humanity from far and near, witnessed works of enormous faith and petty actions of absent faith. It has been a wonderful week. We are now marching west on gentler land still holding surprises and wonderful revelations of the spirit that has forged these places under the Milky Way. A good croissant a day along with "cafe Francais" (half cream and half coffee) in a land without 1% milk or pasteurized cheese is a good start. I am probably sounding too cynical but in a few days I have seen a great contrast between our suffocating protectionism and political correctness and spirited discussion and risk taking as a consistent exercise of human freedom. Are the French better? Hmmm . . . the VAT in my cash register slip will say otherwise along with the forced closings by traditions alien to free enterprise. We shall see.

Routing sign (turn left)

Various surfaces to delight the feet

VILLARET D'APCHIER

Wonderful day with clear blue skies and a cool breeze. Walked about 12 km on rolling hills of the Margeride, a region between the Massif Central and the Aubrac. Vast spaces dominated by short plants, some pine forests, and rocks. Lots of dairy cows. We shared the path with a small herd for a little while. Temperature in the mid to upper 70s made the last portion of the walk (after noon) quite challenging since we walked a great portion on asphalt (most trees are still bare) and shade is not a plentiful commodity. Took time to enjoy the few shady places sitting on cool moss covered granite boulders drinking water or savoring some grapes.

As we walked we have noticed the houses with the windows shut and very few people walking about. It is perhaps a farm community trait that might not be too different from our own farmsteads. It is hard to cross cultural bridges even if several thousand people walk by one's house every year. This increases isolation both ways and leaves exchanges to formula responses that are merely polite ways of hiding.

As bears do in the woods so do we. Taking care of the residue with leaves and dirt covers. Most, if not all, toilet access is restricted to customers for a fee or gratis. In long stretches it is you and the woods taking care of minimizing exposures or offending the bears.

We have changes in our route. Tomorrow we will walk 12 km to Chapelle St. Roch, then on Tuesday we will walk 11 km to St. Alban sur Limagnole. From there we will be transported to Sauges a medieval town remnant for a two day visit and some planning for the rest of the French section. It is a good move more in tune with our physique, walking skill, and ambition. The owners of the refuge here have been most helpful with connections and information.

Narrow, steep, and rough pathways on the edges of the Massif Central

DECAZEVILLE

The cow transfer (transhumaire) is a wonderful Spring ritual that affirms the times and cycles of the land. Perhaps we humans of the Modern persuassion need to consider a seasonal transfer to new or fresher pastures. Our milk and cheese (essence and labor) would then be better. This morning we leave the medieval place of Conques to walk along the floodplain of the Lot River and come to the once thriving mining town of Decazeville. The coal has been gone since 1998 and some post-mining depression still hangs around. We sit at a cafe watching school boys on excursion holding to a common rope and see a picture of community revitalization at its most basic.

Our refuge tonight does not serve dinner so we will visit the superette or the bakery for some delectables plus bottled water for tomorrow's walk. We try to make sure that water is always with us since we consumme 1 liter a day each.

Abbey of St. Foy, Conques
Preserved Medieval Town

108

CAHORS

Surviving rainy days by moving SW toward what would be flatter and warmer lands. The re-planning effort has set us on a course to reach Spain on June 16 and to be in Santiago before July 25. A lot of juggling and a mass of reservation making by cell phone are all done. The rest is for us to walk on time to meet our reservation schedule. Cahors and many small towns on cliffs or valleys in this region owe much to the middle ages as well as to the 100 year war that took the best part of the 14th and 15th centuries. A lot of destruction took place then that was later reprised by the French Revolution and the Counter Reformation. Somehow the churches and some buildings survive. The rivers provided irrigation and power beside drinking water. However, the element often misunderstood is the human one that despite the chaos managed to keep on working and looking forward with confidence in a good outcome. Thus, the ruins and memories serve to underscore not only what was but also what is and even what will be.Tomorrow we will move on to Moissac under hopefully dry skies. It will be the gateway for 11 consecutive days of walking 10 to 16 km per day on a journey that will take us to the edge of the Basque region and the Pyrenees. We are looking forward to seeing a portion of Gascogne just in case the Musketeers still roam the land. There will be lots of fresh fruit (cherries and peaches) but little shade. Gone will be the friendly forests of pine, chestnut, beech, and oak that have often provided fresh shade relief as well as roots to trip over and make the road uneven and tricky. There will be fields of grain and legumes and vegetables.

ERROR: the transhumaire mentioned a few days ago is really the moving of cattle to the higher rather than the lower lands. We have been doing the opposite. From 3,000 ft elevation to 300 ft.In all we are well. No blisters or sprains or breaks.

Our "technique" of wearing compression hose under hiking socks has prevented both blisters and calf cramps although it does not prevent us from feeling the strain of the effort. Nothing like a cool beer at the end of each journey to smooth things out. Although a warm shower did a great job of restoring joy after the Sunday walk in the rain.Moreover, we are happy. There is a lot of joy within and without us to give what the French call "bonheur" and is better translated as "joy of life". The French seem to have less pessimism than Americans or is it the other way around? We are experiencing lots of graciousness and good wishes by people we barely or briefly know. The rain and semi-rural location of our rest station prevented us from walking around Cahors but Moissac awaits with one large cathedral and some Roman and Romanesque treasures. On to the flat lands.

MOISSAC

On the banks of the River Tarn looking at flat land ahead with fruits and vegetables galore. We have been in duck territory for a few days. Almost every dish has duck meat or foie gros in some manner. Quack.Tomorrow starts a 10 days journey to Nogaro from where we will taxi to St Jean Pied de Port at the feet of the Pyrenees for our entry into Spain. The trip is maturing all around us.Visited the 11th century Benedictine abbey of Moissac. Lots of things that were labored by 1,000 monks, partially destroyed, then partially rebuilt, then damaged again, then selectively preserved and publicized. Still the craftsmanship of medieval workers shines through. Wonderful place with a superb cloister that somehow has survived even if some faces in the capitels have lost their noses. Craftsmanship and artisanship. The words still circulate and compel. Have seen many signs advertising artisan breads, artisan butchers, artisan soap, craftsman products and craftsman detailing. Wonder if the words mean the same after 10 centuries. It might be that nothing has changed and the refreshment of terms from the past herald great things. Cathedrals might come back along with abbeys in a new modality. Tomorrow we will be in D'Artagnan territory along with cherry season. Ah, fresh fruit, what a concept. Just bought an "exotic fruit" today at the Municipal Market. Could not resist the temptation of a mango from Mali. Juicy and fleshy and delicious even at 3 euros the kilo. Extravagances must be indulged ever so often for the sake of just feeling pleasure drooling down the chin. Perhaps a man in Mali will buy a Coke with the same joy I received from their mango. Of such things is the world made (or unmade).Every day we do some laundry upon arrival to our station of rest. Most of our clothes are quick drying but still take time to wash and dry. We did a big load today since it had been raining for the past two days. The machines are smaller and take longer however; there is a powerful "green" attitude toward washing machines and detergents that are eco-friendly. Even the superettes proclaim the eco-friendliness of their products. Have not watched or read news from America and all seems to matter very little. Cows and goats as well as chickens and ducks seem to have other concerns.Do not have access to the comments section of this blog. Please e-mail your comments to germancruz@mac.com. We will be glad to hear from you. Please forgive the primitive set up of the blog. It was done in a rush just before departure and some connections and refinement fell by the wayside.See you across the Tarn and the Garonne. Hopefully with a cherry croissant.

POMMEVIC

When the land is flat the walking gets better and faster. Covered 15.5 km at 3 km/hr pace. It could have been faster but we stopped halfway to eat the other "exotic" mango from Mali and do some watching of birds and fishermen in the fluvial plain around the Canal de Garonne and the River Tarn. Most of our traject was on the pathway (tow path) along the southern bank of the canal. Lots of fruit orchards and vegetable farms along with a heron that kept ahead of us like some herald. This definitively is not your rocky and steep pathway of the past two weeks. Lots of people besides pilgrims like us walking and biking under the shadow of huge sycamores of 3 ft plus caliper (waist diameter) set about 12 feet apart by some devoted group. It looks a lot like the Cardinal and White River walkways could look in a certain time. Tomorrow we march on to St. Antoine just 12 km away. We will cross the Garonne River and enter into Armagnac country. Probably stop for lunch and inquiry at Auvillar where the waves of the Albigensian Crusades did some damage and caused reconstructions in Gothic rather than Romaneque style. We might have to take some time to test the local essence of the grape properly distilled. It is also a region of melons but we are a bit early so cherries would have to do.This is our second week of walking and we feel much better although the feet and ankles hold a contrary opinion. No blisters or deep pains in muscles, tendons, and ligaments. We are walking at a comfortable pace with no pretense to athleticism or superior technique. Have met people that "have" to do 30 km or more per day as a practical matter. We are the flatlanders happy to do 12 or 15 happy km. Perhaps the ambition to merely do and keep superior scores is somehow laudable but there is that Aesop fable of the hare and the tortoise to think about.Weather has changed from just a few days ago. It is in the low 80s and our drip dry laundry dries quickly in the full sun. Spain will be much hotter but we will be ready when the time comes.Dinner beckons. Hope duck is not in the menu.

Garonne River Valley

Canal de Goltech (parallel to Garonne River)

Moissac: Hand painted vault at Abbey

ST. ANTOINE D'ARRATZ

Crossed the Garonne River this morning into what is commonly known as the Valley of the Garonne and spent some time at Auvillar Once a great center of the goose quill industry it is now home to great memories and a nuclear power plant (people have not changed color and all children have just one head and two arms). The area is fully agricultural (wheat, sunflowers, fruit orchards, vineyards, geese, and chickens) with little towns making extra living from tourism and history and traffic in the canal.

The weather turned out to be quite hot and most of the walking was on asphalt roads so . . . I got my first blisters. One on the right foot and two on the left. The treatment is easy and it will hopefully promote healing in a few days. There is no problem walking once I get moving. Of course, the moving depends on the body willing to do so.

Tomorrow we will either trot or drag on to Miradoux across wheat fields and whatever weather comes our way.

Auvillar: Wheat Market

In the Land of the Three Musketeers
(D'Artagnan is probably hiding behind the horizon)

MIRADOUX

Left St Antoine at 8am trying to avoid the late morning and mid afternoon sun. Had partial success in the coolness of the morning fog but after about 10:30 the sun decided to cook the wheat fields along with anybody caught in their vicinity. Luckily we had a nice trek through some chestnut woods (about 1 km) before we marched along waist high wheat to our final destination or just there. Entering towns usually calls for a climb up a hill (colline) at a high heart rate made often worst by the heat. Most towns were built on dominant views of the surrounding countryside for defensive purposes (it does not matter that we come in peace 10 centuries later). Just before our woods sojourn we had made a mistake in following the signs (yes, like in baseball there are signs). One must watch for three stripes of white/red/white painted on walls, trees, posts, and other places) and a farmer came honking after us to get back to the right road. He was working on his cherry orchard when he saw us. We got about two pounds of freshly picked cherries and a wonderful expression of kindness. From the wheat field we could see Miradoux in the distance perched atop a hill, teasing us trekking through the undulating terrain. We could see a narrow strip of red clay along a pine forest. The closer we got, the more evident the role of the steep clay road in getting us to town. Then we climbed for half an hour on this natural and topogaphic cardiac exercise machine under a rather hot sun. I probably broke some sweat glands and Karen reached high tones of red in her cheeks. The owner of our way station welcomed us with a very cold beer and lemon drink that put out many fires in our system. The walking is not a problem but the heat and the absence of prolonged shade is a problem. We pass many ponds and swimming pools that seem to call us like the mermaids calling the sailors in the Odissey. The Garonne River that we crossed yesterday is really a line (the Midi) that divides France into North and South just like the Ohio River. The agricultural South with large estates and strong independent character had its own tongue (Occitan or Langue d'Oc) and manners. The industrial North had refinement, palatial intrigue, religious power, academia, and its own language that eventually became what we know today as French. Any similarity with the USA is merely the same. Our Civil War became in France a war of religion and a revolution highly focused on an urban thematic where "country people" were either oafish or untrustworthy by reason of their independence. Of course, this is highly simplified but marching through wheat and harvesting cherries are not urban activities. The charm displayed by the cherry farmer and our host speak of gentility often found more in Charleston than Boston.Tomorrow we will try a 15 km trot. The blisters are responding well to treatment with a "magic" product we got at the pharmacy in Auvillar. Despite the heat we are enjoying this. Just saw the sonograms of my daughter's baby and it might be good that at some future time he be told the crazy walk of his/her grandparents into D'Artagnan country on the way to Santiago. The Musketeers might be fiction but the exhaustion in our bodies is real along with the joy of this adventure.

LECTOURE

A good stage of 12.5 km that got extended by about 2 km in our efforts to find our guest house in a town that has little faith in signage, and since it is Sunday, everything is closed including the Tourist Office (on a high visit day). C'est la France. The law controls how long and when stores are open by reason of decreed rest periods for workers and other Gallic eccentricities.Wheat to the right, wheat to the left, melons ahead and cyclists everywhere. Far too much spandex for my taste. If equipment makes the sport, then cycling is above all. The medical report is good. Using the healing plastic skin bandages is great. Karen has blister on the side of an ankle that was giving her some trouble today. We will rest it tonight and probably put a patch of plastic skin on it. She has been a very brave walker and a most engaging person to all. It seems like graciousness is currency all around the planet (with the possible exception of Washington D.C.). On Saturday under a hot sun we walked through woods and a wheat field seeking a shady spot to sit and rest awhile. On top of the hill a farmer had built a shelter, put a picnic table under it with several 2 liter bottles of water, a few glasses, an invitation to satisfy the thirst, and a little metal can for donations at will. We saw him later weeding his vegetable garden but he refused to acknowledge our calls. In the great scope of things this is a small act by a single man but to us was a very joyful event. From our seats at the picnic table we could see a wonderful panorama of wheat fields, oak woods, melon farms, a few vineyards, and a large pond under a clear blue sky. From our hearts we saw generosity and love. Lectoure sits atop a long hill and looks like a battleship from a distance. We saw it from about 5 km away but did not know how arduous it would be to reach its central plaza. We walked about 3 km to the very bottom of the hill, then huffed and puffed for a very long and steep 2 km to reach the cathedral and then walk all over trying to find our guest house. Once in the house we were "honored" with a room for two at the top of three stories of steps. We will probably shower and snooze a bit before dinner at 7:30 pm. Started as a Gaul town, Lectoure became a Roman colony and in the Middle Ages rose to prominence as a commercial center. It had two lords: the bishop and the counts of Armagnac (the area produces Cognac). In the late 1400s the city was destroyed by forces from Albi (remember the Albi-gensians?) who killed the count but the city recovered and it is still a large center of regional commerce. We will have a chance to test some Cognac tonight. The walk to Marzolan might help clear our heads tomorrow.Have not experienced much silence yet. Our march is marked by the incessant pliant chant of doves, the ever present voice of coo-coo birds with participation from all kinds of song birds. The wind plays a role also as well vehicular sounds and church bells announcing the time. Perhaps in Spain. Karen is coming out of the shower, so it is my turn.

MARSOLAN

After some roundabout on medieval streets we found our way out of the historic fortified perimeter into the industrial area and down to the River Gers at a point early in its course. Walking by the side of a busy road was not our idea of fun despite warnings to avoid the traditional path . . . so we took the traditional route and endured a 30 minute walk through the floodplain and a rather well attended mosquito convention. We have been craving for some insect repellent but we hit towns without pharmacy or the one they have is closed for the day or the hour of our arrival. There is no such thing as a 24 hour service anything in France. After the heroic battle of the mosquito, we hit open country under a blazing sun taking advantage of every shaded spot to take a water break. The topography is rather gentle with only two or three cardio workouts (we might be getting in better condition climbing wise) and very pleasant flat sections. The hamlet of Marsolan is just a place with no more than 20 or 30 houses and less than 100 people. There is no cafe or bar and our guest house is the "big" place. As before, since Moissac, the hills are alive with the sound of wheat or the quaking of poplar leaves. The cooing of doves is often overwhelming which has hunters salivating over a great season to come. Some days I would like to call all the cats in the area against them but they would probably just shrug their shoulders in a feline Gallic gesture of indifference. It might well be that all cats in France are unionized or pacifist. After several days of avoiding all things duck we were cornered last night and surrendered to a wonderful dinner of roasted duck (confit) with a nice green salad and an almond torte. There was soup also (pumpkin and squash with yellow vegetables). Magnificent. The weight loss plan hit a small bump since there is a lot of sweating every journey and the loss is soon caught up.Tomorrow we will hop over to La Romieu, an old teaching abbey town that might have one or two open pharmacies and other services. In our American way we think and expect all merchants open all the time for our convenience. France might be more about privilege than convenience. Just like BSU and similar enterprises.We arrived early to our rest station and have spent the afternoon doing laundry the old fashioned way since using washers and much less dryers hereabouts requires an advanced degree in the dark sciences. It is only so far that two shirts and a pair of underwear go in this heat.Tomorrow we will step on an old Roman road for a few meters. This area was dotted with Roman camps keeping the empire safe from Gauls, Normans, Germans and other original inhabitants.May you all have a wonderful week. We are trying to do that here. It rained a bit during our journey yesterday but it kept the sun from shining directy on us. Happy trails.

LA ROMIEU

Did a rather fast walk from Marsolan this morning. Rain was in the forecast and after hearing a rather heavy downpour around 5 am we were ready for a good soaking today. Yet, we had a cloudy day with high humidity instead. Left our host station before 8 am and got here right at noon after some rest stops for water and toilet. The blisters are in a friendly cooperative mood for which we are grateful. Tomorrow we will hit Condom where we expect to find a pharmacy to replenish our supply of Compeed and get some arnica gel to reduce inflamation and bring about geater relief. Our walking is fine but with some healing it could help us move faster. La Romieu (from the Gascon "Roumiou" = Pilgrim) dates from a convent founded in the early 14th century that soon became an abbey (1313) that fell under the protection of Arnaud d'Aux, member of the family of the Counts of Armagnac. He became bishop and then cardinal serving as chamberlain for two popes (Clement V and John XXII) while holding the papal seat for two years until the election of his cousin John XXII. The abbey was kind of a seminary, convent, technical school. Protestant forces destroyed the abbey, burned the records, and generally pillaged and ransacked both the abbey and the town.The area is a high producer of prunes with hillsides covered for several kilometres with orchards of plums that stand like armies on both sides of the road. It is like walking along a large military review. The remnant of the abbey has a cloister of Gothic style that is well preserved and restored along with a medieval herb garden carefully annotated with the various medicinal uses of each plant. There is also a large botanical garden just 500 meters from the abbey. It is a beautiful place with a very large collection of roses. Large and bountiful in all manner of habits. The climate in the region is very Mediterranean and encourages a rich and diverse palette of plants. This makes me think of adding more roses to my garden and fighting bugs, soil, and weather more effectively. Some of the orange varieties are awesome. Condom promises to be a great treat (as well as treatment). It has one of the top 20 gothic cathedrals in the world. It will be a walking challenge (15.5 km) but we should get there in 5 or 6 hours (8 AM to 2 PM) since the terrain is kindly undulating. We hope the forecasted rain does not fall on us. Humid is ok but rainy is truly a mess since it puts us in an urgent need to do laundry and dry clothes where such activity is hard to manage at best. Let's hope for the best. We could very well have a journey like today with a series of open field marches followed by traversing of dark and thick oak forests. They are like tunnels but quite fresh and welcoming. La Romieu is known as the "City of Cats" by reason of a medieval story where cats saved by a young woman (Angeline) were able to rid the city of rats after most cats had been consumed during a famine. There is a bust of Angeline with a cat like face in front of City Hall. See you in Condom.

CONDOM

We thought it would be a stormy day; however, it rained cats and dogs and probably ducks last night. The day began overcast with high humidity and stayed so for all morning and afternoon. The paths were muddy and slippery with that yellow sandy clay that really sticks to the bottom of shoes and forms good adobe material when mixed with fresh cut grass and hay. The shoes get heavy with clumps holding on for the ride and then the pants receive their mud bath to give us the appearance of escaped prisoners from a ditch digging detail. Yet, we managed to do about 16.5 km in 5 hours with a couple of stops for revitalization.The first stop was just 5 km into the stage. The village of Castlenau sur l'Auvignon sit on the saddle of a long hill. It was a center of the French Resistance during WW II. It had a lot of fighters who bedeviled the Nazis with constant sabotage and guerrilla action. Many were killed for their actions and a nearby village was massacred in an attempt to find the Resistance fighters. We kind of stopped and sat in silence to honor the heroes and the place. La Romieu (the village just before) has a monument to Resistance fighters with a special place for those murdered by the Gestapo. The war might be over but the memories linger. Places are consecrated (made holy) by the selfless actions of people with integrity. Perhaps other kind of human action might also have consecrating power.Our second stop was less momentous. We stopped for lunch after searching for a bench or a suitable rock. Eventually we came upon a culvert wall and shared an apple, some water, and a mint. We had found the grocery store closed in La Romieu and forgot to pilfer bread from the breakfast table. Some stages have little commercial support between destinations. We always carry one liter of water, some fruits, canned fish, bread and other goodies but this time we got bushwacked by the wacky operating hours of several businesses in France. Condom is a city of about ten thousand people. We finally found an open pharmacy and a fruit grocer. The cathedral is huge. It was the last one built in the Languedocian style. Construction started in 1507 and continued for one hundred years. Its complex became a prison during the Revolution. Condom sits at the heart of Gascogne and it is the major center for Armagnac. We could not visit the museum of Armagnac for lack of time rather than lack of will. There is only so much one can do after a day of sloshing through muddy paths. Our dinner tonight will have desserts that use Armagnac.We will continue tomorrow toward Lamothe in what might be another sweatty slosh across woods and wheatfields. Hope it does not rain.

LASSERRE DE HAUT

12.2 km through forests mostly. Long green tunnels with slippery clay base. Last night's rain turned pathways into small creeks and today we march on mud that sticks to shoes with stubborn insistence. For a while it felt like walking with snow shoes. Even though the day was quite hot and the last 3 km were over asphalt roads, we arrived at our rest station just ahead of a storm. This puts a crimp on our washing and drying plans but it is good to watch thunder rather than walk under it.

Pont d'Artigues over Osse River

Most of the area is vineyards and sunflower farming with the inevitable wheat field. Few towns, just farms and places to stay. We are honored today by our age and love of opera with assignment to the "Carmen" room. It is an 18' x 18' room decorated in themes of bullfghting. There is even a papier mache bull's head in one corner. Ole!

We splurged yesterday at the fruit and vegetable market and bought a melon(â,¬3.50). It was grown locally and it was the size of 16" softball. Today we had it for lunch at an old Roman bridge over the River L'Osse. Delicious. Then we pondered about the memories held by the bridge over 21 centuries. People of all types passing through on the way somewhere. If bridges could talk.

Had a Gascogne dinner last night that started with an appetizer of green apple liqueur and armagnac. Superb. We broke all dietary laws and probably pay dearly with our sweat in the folowing days . . . but you only live twice and the spirit of Gascogne must be indulged.

The rain has ended and now the hot sun has returned. We have almost 5 more hours of sunshine and a little laundry work beckons.

LAMOTHE

Ambled for 7 hours through vineyards and wheatfields as well as the now usual green tunnel. No cities. Just farmstands and the humming echo of nearby highways. The highway is about 10 km away but it feels like it is closer. Mechanical noise pollution is very pervasive and powerful. Enjoyed a farmer's market early on the walk and indulged in "fraises du bois" (small strawberries), white peaches from Spain, a local melon (about 16" softball size) and then hit the bakery for fresh apricot beignets and bread. Had the melon for lunch sitting on a log on the edge of a woods with a view of acres and acres of vineyards. Did not have wine but relished fresh potable water from the town's fountain we had passed en route. Life is now quite simple. Our rest stop is full. A mix of French and German walkers plus two Americans who walk "tenderly". The Camino has about 4 evident categories of walkers. There are the high power ones who tackle long distance (30 km) as a quest and care dearly for distance and time. Then there are the middle power ones who do 20 km every day with time for some exploration or stop for refreshment along the way. Then there is us who walk slow, stop a lot, question a lot and are happy to do no more than 15km (if necessary). We are the "tender" walkers. Then there are the "escargots" or snail walkers who do short distances of less than 10 km and hang around the rest stops to delight in the exchange of anecdotes. It takes all kinds.In walking the Camino one must pay attention to the signs. Taking a wrong turn or getting lost is not fun when you are tired and the weather is hot. Also, along the path there are signs that unequivocally state private property boundaries, no fishing, no hunting, no touching, no entering, no picking, no stopping. These are universal products of our need for ownership of space and the communication of that need very much like boundary marking set by urination in the wild by wild creatures. Perhaps there is an affinity between dogs marking territory and humans marking ownership. Of course this has been investigated in scholarly material that it might be my delight to check out later. Karen is learning the secrets of French washing machines. It is a dark art that requires much patience and Karen is a great pupil. So much for today.

Eauze: Bullring (Spain must be near)

Eauze: Church of St. Luperc

Built in 1521 by Benedictines using rubble from Roman ruins.

LE HAGET

Walked 15.5 km in nice weather from 7:30 to 2:30 with a long stop halfway at Eauze. A rather long city with a central plaza under remodeling but a very vibrant business district. Had a Perrier with lemon syrup and watched the local color. Visited the cathedral also under repair and remodeling. Nicely done repairs to a building that mixes Gothic and late Romanesque (kind of becoming more aware of styles, periods, and techniques). The city is the "official capital" of Armagnac and they let you know it. Lots of pride and big push for all things Gascon. As a matter of fact the Camino runs today through the finest vineyards in the region with the "domaine" houses (major wineries) very much evident on the hilltops. They stand rather like castles overseeing the acreage of the realm. The walk takes longer but one comes to appreciate the labor and pride that goes into every bottle. Thought rather impudently of our students as products of our "domaine" with appropriate labels and harvest dates. Getting from Lamothe to Eauze one walks on an old rail way. It felt like walking on the Cardinal Walkway except tree cover here is quite mature and creates the green tunnel effect I mentioned before. Encountered many people walking and jogging besides us "pilgrims".Our rest station tonight is a farm owned by a British young couple who have been in France for 10 years. They have free range Gascon pigs (about 50) plus free range chickens, penned rabbits, and a large assortment of vegetables. The regional market buys out their product. They have no relational connection to France other than a place to do what they wanted to do. I guess freedom to do is a basic element of happiness. We get a room for ourselves.Last night we slept in a dormitory and Mrs Cruz was not too happy about the conditions. The place was run by a German young man and provided a lot of basic comfort but it had "rules" that somehow betrayed a German ordered view rather than French chaos. The discomfort started when we arrived and our name was not in the list. I had called on June 1 to make reservations. The next rest station was almost 3 km farther and we had reached our limit for the day. Eventually all was settled in 3 languages with much gesturing. We shared a dormitory room with three other people. The entire place uses IKEA products down to the dinnerware. It was odd to have this touch of modernity in a region that celebrates the old styles.Tomorrow we march on to Nogaro which closes out our walking in France and places us next week in Spain.

Greenwich Meridian

NOGARO

The final walking stage in France. 15 km over many hills and dales. Forded a shallow creek while Karen did her Indiana Jones walk across a 14" wide slab. Two people, one obstacle, two ways of dealing with it.

Have truly tested ourselves over a wide range of situations. We come out with a better understanding of the land, the people, and ourselves. Have not seen American TV or read American news for almost 4 weeks. It feels less urgent and enables us to focus on the issues truly at hand like health, rest, food. Not that America does not matter but that in the scope of things this walk is more important than whatever happens in Washington, New York, Muncie or elsewhere. In these weeks we have met a lot of people who are surprised to meet Americans from such a far and unknown place like Indiana. Only once have I been asked about Obama. In fact, more people ask about agriculture and industry (perhaps it is the nature of the region) than even sports. People know about the East and West coasts but truly little or nothing about our flyover country. There has been much talk about education, cheese, architecture, medieval history, cherries, wine, and bread. Little or not talk about baseball or sports other than soccer, rugby, and petanque (kind of a bocce game with steel balls). In all it has been a rather strange sojourn. Our bodies ache but our hearts and minds are alive with wonderful feelings and memories. Spain might beckon but France is ever alive in us.

Had a wonderful dinner last night at our farm hospedage. Grilled pork chops, fingerling yellow potatoes, green salad, homemade bread, and a bowl of raspberries with cream. Everything produced within 100 feet of our table except for the red wine that came from the area. Magnificent.

Tomorrow we will be transported to St Jean Pied de Port for our preparation of the entry to Spain. It will be busy and exciting.

ST JEAN PIED DE PORT

We have been here for two days preparing for today's foray into Spain. A transport service will take us to Logrono where we will put feet to ground in what will be one month of marching across northern Spain to Santiago de Compostela. St Jean is a "gateway" city which might mean a place in constant welcoming mode. Two major streets and lots of restaurants, stores, and hostels wrapped in a Basque identity (every place has a French and a Basque name). From our hotel window we can see the old city wall and the slopes of the Pyrenees with their grazing clearings and terrace farming along with rather steep grades made more for viewing than walking. In town the contrasts are striking. Old men with berets sipping coffee or tea or harder stuff speaking Basque while the background music is American rock or its European equivalent. Tourists (Camino walkers and non-walkers) gawking or trying to make sense of the carnival atmosphere. It is definitively a different part of France. Sheep abounds in the hills and at the dining table along with Basque specialties often meant for a rich and more intense lifestyle. The vehicular traffic through St Jean is amazing on top of the human crowd. It is more like a Modern version of a siege camp. Spain will have no choice but to surrender to these expectant and eager troops with backpacks and walking rods and batons. It has been raining or drizzling for the past two days but the crowd just flows and ebbs. SE France has been hit hard by flash floods with a lot of destruction. This area has only lots of rain and people framed by Basque identity and politics. The move to Logrono rather than a climb to Roncesvalles and subsequent descent to Pamplona responds to our desire for a flatter terrain and some respect for our feet and knees. It would take us between 8 and 9 hours to reach Roncesvalles just to share a dormitory with about 50 to 100 snorers. Logrono gives us an opportunity to get away from the madding crowd as well as the rain. Not that we are quite sane but there are levels of madness we have yet to reach. Spent most of the past two days scheduling the walk through Spain with calls to reserve space at rest stops and investigation of routes and conditions. This had been done in general ways back in Muncie but we all know that when the plan hits the ground everything is in play as if there has never been a plan at all. Now we have a "working" plan that will help us greatly, all things being equal. Napoleon and Charlemagne crossed into Spain at Roncesvalles, we will go by car. Each army has different means. The goal is Santiago and we intend to get there in good health and decent shape. Spain beckons.

PROFILES OF SPAIN

Le Chemin de St. Jacques or the Way of Puy becomes El Camino Francés or the French Way once across the Pyrenees. Then the land sort of undulates less precipitously than in France. The ground is sandier and less muddy. Distances are the same but heat increases. This year Spain is under assualt by Saharan hot winds that elevate temperatures and cause much discomfort without streams of indoor air conditioned spaces. The ceiling fans are merely air blenders producing a smoothie of sticky and hot environment that is great for drying laundry and drinking beer with lemonade. Spain is more urban but still has vast areas of farmland. Mostly vineyards and small vegetable plots framed by large fields of wheat, barley and melons. We will also have vastly different food since the refuges and hostals do not have food service and small restaurants, bars and cafes will now entertain our appetite. There will be regional specialties as well as the traditional ham and cheese sandwiches (thin slice of "serrano" ham and an equally thin slice of sheep milk cheese in a long bun). However, red or Rioja wine will flow like water from a faucet. Just like in France, hours of business operation subject to local custom and Summer hours.

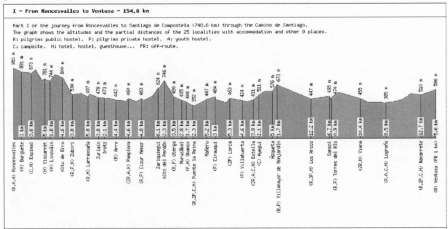

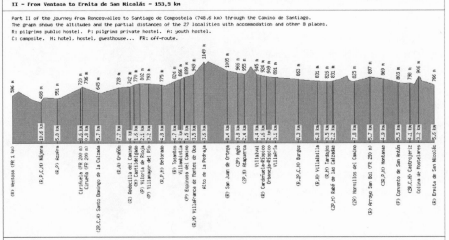

Overall, people will be the same as in France with great interest on the soccer world cup and local festivals. We will be crossing several regions that were formally kingdoms or principalities with

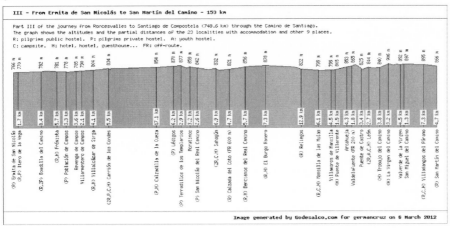

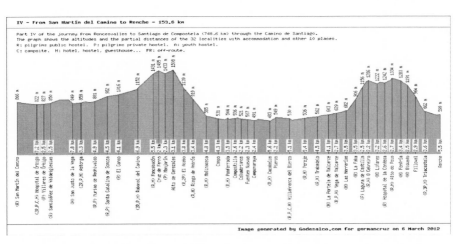

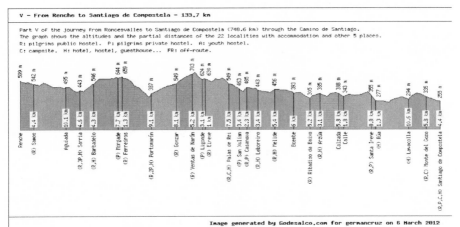

strong regional identity and very mixed historical narratives across time. The common language might be Spanish (Castillian) and faith (Roman Catholicism) but the ancient local language still rules. Somehow, Spain is held by thin bonds of nationhood and a common larger vision that is hard to discern at first. The regional character dominates everyday life and it is best to talk about weather and sports than politics and economics (poverty is apparent and dire at times). The ancient blends with the new but not always in a good fitting manner. More like adaptive reuse than historical engagement. Certainly, a lot more churches than in France and large public spaces like river walks, plazas, or parks.

Of course, opinions of Spain from guidebooks and travel blogs will be subject to change upon experience and further inquiry. We still have about 500 miles to walk before reaching Santiago and each step out of about 880,000 must give individual account of itself on real time in a real place. Spain will be shown to us on a daily basis. The ancient history and the brave deeds of soldiers and kings will blend with the current lives of people to become either background or foreground of what this peninsula has been or

can be. Certainly, there are scars from wars and factional poses (struggles); however, there is a lot in common that is not easily discounted. Seems like the contemporary struggle is played more in soccer fields rather than the politics of old land and regions. Barcelona (Catalunya)) versus Real Madrid (Capital City) or Osasuna (Basque) versus Granada (Andalucia). History is what someone writes independent of individual lives but every Sunday, the country examines itself in the outcome of games and to the victors belong the spoils or at least the headlines. Interestingly, the national team has a large and very important contingent of players from Catalunya, once the stronghold of independence movements and opponents (Nationalists) to the conservative central government (Fascists).

In all, Spain looms from atop Roncesvalles as a very complex aggregation rather than a smooth mix. Our encounter along a rather narrow line (slice) walked by thousands over 10 centuries will be a brief sampling of a modern nation that once owned and ruled the world (Treaty of Tordesillas). The cathedrals as well as farmers and merchants will speak loud and clear. Right under the soil and in the culture there is a heritage of Visigoths, Celts,

Romans, Moors, Basques, Castillians and various local tribes. From the window of our transport between St. Pied de Port and Logroño there is evidence of modernity attached to tradition and old fabric. The semi trucks that carry goods and vegetables from Andalucia to Europe are not different than the armies that shared the New World with the continent. Most certainly, we will be walking in or in between old and new over the next days. Unlike the French portion of the walk, we will be encountering more urban areas as well as less green surfaces (at least until we reach Galicia).

Diet wise we expect significant changes caused by local customs of late night dining (9 to 10 PM) as well as local fare. Summer sun sets around 10PM. Our walk through France feasted us on regional cuisine of a delightful nature. Spain will offer a different view with probably "tapas" (snacks) as the normal fare since the demand of daily marches will preclude late night food consumption. Bodies need rest before starting walk at 7AM or so. Bars will offer "tapas" after 6 PM and most are quite satisfying. Another possible solution will be taking lunch at local bars or cafes when available. Somehow, our stomachs will survive. Surely, local markets will offer plenty of fresh fruit.

LOGROÑO/NAVARRETE

Spain is definitively a different kettle of fish. Arrived at Logrono after 2PM, took a walk in the central city as is our custom. Everything was closed until 5PM (Summer Hours) except for some bar/grills and a few candy stores (surprising high number). Sat at a terrace to sip an orange drink and watch the pigeons before returning to the hotel to take a siesta until a more decent hour. After 5PM the place came alive. Went to the market to buy some fruit, tried to have early (6PM) dinner but no dinner served until 8PM. So we did tapas (small bar counter goodies/snacks) with a generous helping of Rioja red wine. Right in front of us a roving mariachi band (about 12 musicians) regaled us with a two song set. So dinner and show for less than the price of a full meal. Not bad.Logrono is the capital of the Autonomous Community of La Rioja (Spain has several of this type of communities distinguished by ethnic or regional character as the price of what passes for national unity). It has 145,000 inhabitants and its industry is centered around the very fine and much liked wine produced in the region. Around the center city there are various pedestrian ways that contain many "tasting" or "sampling" bars where one can explore the various products from the many wineries in the region. The bars close at 2AM and we experienced their impact in our hotel with noisy revelers either in the street or getting to their rooms. Shortly after, the street sweepers move in with their small pressurized water and brush machines and it is all clean for the morning rush. There is a great emphasis on public sector jobs, specially street repair and cleaning as well as garbage collection. People in green uniforms are everywhere. Minimum wage is 9 euros (about US$11.70) with benefits.From Logroño we walked along a couple of long avenues to a greenway to a large park to a greenway connector to a large lake surrounded by a regional park. It was a good 6 km walk all together. There were a lot of people

walking, jogging, biking, fishing, or simply sitting out in the sun. I thought of a similar connection between Muncie CBD and Prairie Creek. There was a cafe with nice service as well as a full serve restaurant. Radical.The rest of the way to Navarrete took us through soft hills planted with vineyards. The red sandy clay soil is rich with pebbles (perhaps more pebbles than soil). We might have to sample some of the product of these carefully tended vineyards.Tomorrow we will walk 16 km to Najera which doubles Navarrete in population (7,000 people). There is a small climb but it comes after our lunch break. It is really weird to walk into a town during the early afternoon and see nobody in the streets. It is like towns in a western movie when the baddies come to town. Hope Clint Eastwood rides with us.

Santiago Matamoros (St. James the oorslayer) at City Gate

NAJERA

Good walk to Ventosa (the windy place) in a cloud covered morning with a strong and cold face wind that flowed through my new hat. The cap offers no sun protection except to the top. Path displayed the pebbles that are mixed with the soil throughout the region. Stepping got difficult for my left foot due to the blister and its "extensions" (my foot is a suburban expansion theatre). Every time I stepped on a stone it felt as if a needle went through the foot. At Ventosa (7.6 km from Navarrete) the foot hurt too much to walk, we stopped at a cafe, and the barkeep took pity and recommended a taxi ride and some rest. So, after a 15 minute ride we arrived in Najera to the joy of my feet. Rubbed arnica gel on the feet and sprayed the blister area with antiseptic before applying a Compeed patch. Feel better already.Najera was a Roman stronghold that was later occupied by the Visigoths and the Moors until liberated in the late 10th century by the king of Pamplona and Navarre to become the seat of the Kingdom of Navarre after the destruction of Pamplona by the Moors. It retained its prominence until the 17th century and it is today a vigorous tourist center in what is called the High Rioja where vineyards give way to wheat fields.As we settled in our rooms there was a loud noise of people singing and marching bands in the promenade just outside the hotel. There is an encounter of "peñas". Which are associations of young and old for travel and amusement (kind of freeform Elks Club type groups). They danced and drank beer and wine displaying handkerchiefs and vests and shirts with their particular colors. Afterwards they continued to parade on the major streets under the watchful eye of the "Civil Protection" (Guardia Civil) or local police (un-armed guards) and the bemused look of residents. Tonight they will hold a concert, board their busses and go home. It is a large, open air event mixing college and middle age participants. Would there be a lot of drinking? Yes. Would there be a lot of fun? Yes. Would someone be scandalized? No. The event seems to burn off a lot of energy and tension from final exams. Elsewhere, students hold rallies and build bonfires (minor contributors to global warming but large stress relief events). Thinking that a giant bonfire and dance would be a wonderful event at CAP. Of course, having fun is not a renewable resource. The planet cannot tolerate such non-sense.The sandy red clay of La Rioja has also nurtured a clay pottery industry centered mostly around Navarrete where there are seven to ten large kilns. Some of the works are extraordinarily large or quite intricate and displayed proudly on window sills and large spaces to hold flowering and foliage plants.Walked yesterday for some time with a German financial officer who has just quit his banking job in Ireland to walk the Camino. We did a lot of comparison between USA and Europe until we got trapped by the thematic of my book on "Theology of the Land" that keeps bouncing in my thoughts and notes. He offered some excellent comments and promised a greater contribution via e-mail later. I was quite stimulated and felt less the stress of walking. A week of relative solitude and writing once back in Muncie will help advance greatly the subject. Might have to write in several languages since the input has been vast from various camps. As I write, the music from the various bands resounds through town. Dinner is at 9PM so the music might last until then with more to come later in the night.Some of the music is rather good and invites some dancing response.Tomorrow we will arrive to Santo Domingo de la Calzada, a major point in the development of the Camino that has been designated by both UNICEF and the European Union as a "Patrimony of Mankind". I wonder if Muncie could be proclaimed "Patrimony of the Industrial Age".

SANTO DOMINGO
DE LA CALZADA

Mostly windy and kind of cold day. Seems like we are followed by mild weather with traces of early Spring. Somehow Summer is held captive by clouds and stubborn cold weather. Of course, we might be talking about merciless sun in a few days that will also prevent us from sitting in an open air cafe. Santo Domingo de la Calzada is named after Domingo de Viloria who lived in the early half of the 11th century. The "calzada" refers to the paved road built by the saint. It derives from the Spanish "calzado" for shoe or shoed. Thus a shoed road is a paved path. After unsuccessfully trying to enter two monasteries, he became a hermit and dedicated himself to helping pilgrims walking over the old Roman roads that came on the way to Santiago. This concern led him to clear and pave the road, build a hostal and a hospital for pilgrims that became the nucleus of a new town later named after him. His remains are buried in the cathedral in a massive and impressing tomb carved in alabaster under a Gothic style mausoleum. Many miracles have been attributed to Santo Domingo. The foremost relates to the fate of a young man walking to Santiago with his parents in the 12th century. When he refused the endearments of a young woman daughter of an innkeeper, she accused him of theft and under the laws of the time he was sentenced to death and hanged. The parents came to claim the body but instead they found the son who told them how Santo Domingo had saved his life. The parents went to the Corregidor (local judge) to tell him of the miracle. The Corregidor laughed at them saying their son was not more alive than the cooked rooster and hen he was ready to eat for dinner. Immediately, the rooster and hen jumped from the plate and the rooster began to crow. There is a cove at the cathedral right in front of the tomb of Santo Domingo where a white rooster and hen are held. The pair is changed every month. Yesterday at Najera we had opportunity to admire the stork nests atop the towers of the Cathedral of Santa Maria la Real. Very interesting masses of twigs high up on the towers with awkward birds ignoring our presence below. The nuns were rehearsing their choir and we could not see the inside of the church until after 8PM mass which is late for us walkers who need rest rather than evening Romanesque vaults and arches. The cathedral has several rather awesome guilded "retablos" (altars) carved by 13th century artists. They rise 3 stories with intricate carvings loaded with images (painted and sculpted) coated or painted in gold. It almost hurts the eyes and confounds the mind to engage their narrative. The cathedral museum is really a treasure house of ecclesiastical art in precious metals and exquisitively carved and painted (porcelain finished) images of saints. One wonders in awe at mastery and faith that made all these things possible in cultures and times where long periods of peace were often rare. The local gathering of "peñas" ended after 2AM with rockets and uproars. This morning we were able to see some of the revellers still ambling through town looking for breakfast or a friendly pillow. We just cannot party that hard. Three glasses of Rioja wine and we are pillow food. It is not so much maturity as old age and tired bodies. Tomorrow we head to Castildelgado (narrow or thin castle). It was once a big center of chocolate production.

CASTILDELGADO

Rather comfortable walk under cool weather and over soft hills. We walked on the High Rioja with a landscape that resembles a blanket of color patches with various tonalities of green and brown sprinkled with red poppies. No more vineyards. It is time for wheat and other cereals along with beets and table vegetables. Three quarters of the way we came upon a tall pylon that marks the border with Castille and Leon. Really it is a regional border marker for the largest agglomeration of provinces that create an autonomous community that includes 9 provinces: Burgos, Palencia, Leon, Castille, Segovia, Salamanca, Avila, Soria, Valladolid and Zamora. We will only cross three of them (Burgos, Palencia, and Leon) but after that we will be 155 km from Santiago. This area is in general the historic core of Spain and the Camino has been the key linkage that unified it. In the far past the region was settled by Visigoths from which it has been called the Gothic Country. It is a land of soft undulating hills and wide valleys rich in cultivation of grains and vegetables to the point that it is the breadbasket of Spain. It was also the stage for the Reconquista or recovery of the land from the Moors in the 15th century. In many ways it is a key component of the Hispanic realm and now a big player in the economy of the European Union. Castildelgado is a very small town, rather a hamlet on the side of both the Camino and a large East-West national route. Thus, we are staying at what can best be called a truck stop. It is a place that offers a bar, a restaurant, and very nice rooms with bathroom. From the windows we can see fields and hills beyond the trucks from all parts of Spain and Europe. There was even one from Saint Gobain that somehow establishes a linkage with Muncie. A big advantage here is a dining room that caters to truckers rather than gastronomic explorers. Of course, the official dinner time is 9PM with a more formal menu offering but there are tapas and bocadillos (small sandwiches) at the bar at any time. We had a big lunch of paella, roast chicken, salad, and flan so we will eat some fruit in our room, watch the Spain vs Honduras soccer game in the World Cup and fall asleep at a good hour. The sun sets at almost 10PM but we set earlier. There is only so much fun a pair of old walking codgers can have. Somehow we seem to be less tired as we walk. Could be that our form has improved or the topography has flattened. In any case we are enjoying the journey a lot more. Spain offers more small cities with refreshments and sitting opportunities than the largely farm driven context of France. Today we had a stop midway at a small town (Grañon) with several cafes and a wonderful bakery operated by a mother and her daughters. We bought some goodies and were treated to fresh baked cookies after engaging in animated conversation.The Camino is truly an international way. Today we met a couple from Wales (Cardiff) who walked with us for a couple of kilometers. Later we walked with a couple from Canada (Calgary), and conversed at various times with two young women from Sweden (Stockholm) who needed some advice on the care of muscular stress. There is a lot of sharing of experiences and great curiosity for places of origen as well as destinations after the walk. Cordiality and generosity envelops the entire experience.Tomorrow we will march 11 km to Belorado that moves us closer to the Montes de Oca (wilderness of the geese) that were the halfway point in the old pilgrimages rife with highwaymen until the Knights Templar took on policing the area. They seemed to be the medieval answer to the question of protection. Kind of a state trooper regiment or ghostbusters. Who are you going to call? 1- 800 - T E M P L A R, that is the call. Might have to get a chain mail shirt and a broad sword.

The Montes de Oca have a family linkage to the Cruz line since my grandmother's maiden was Montesdeoca which betrays a provenance way back in the roots of a family tree. I might not find a relative from the 16th century but might feel my gradmother walking in the memory of these thickets and hills.

BELORADO

Sunny day with no clouds and a bright blue sky. Walking through cereal fields without shade somehow makes the progress faster. Left Castildelgado around 8:30 after breakfast with the trucker crowd and reached Belorado at noon with brief stops at Viloria de Rioja and Villamayor del Rio for refreshments. We are either getting better or time is standing still.

Traffic on El Camino is getting heavier. This morning we were passed by about 30 people on their way to places further away than our modest daily trek. Japanese young couple trying hard to communicate in Spanish but settling for English. German man trying to convey excitement about somebody else wearing the same type of hat (me). English couple practicing their basic Spanish. Lots of young people walking past us and wishing: "buen camino" while others just say "hola" or wave.

Staying today at refuge owned by a Dutch/ Nicaraguan couple. Karen loves it. She looks quite comfortable in the terricloth bathrobe provided for our comfort while at the refuge. The bathroom is down the hall.

We had expected warmer weather but it has been kind of cool except for today. It is the first full day of Summer and it appears as if the weather has suddenly changed toward the seasonal normal or usual. Hope it does not get too hot.

Slowly we make our way to Burgos. Then it will be toward Leon, and afterwards to Santiago. This 3-way split helps us get some sort of dimension on the planning and execution parts.

In about a month we will be in Santiago. What an awesome thought. Who would have "thunk" it.

Lots of stork nests in the various high towers in town. The big birds stand in their pile of twigs probably thinking high thoughts or wondering if we can think standing on one leg like them.

VILLAFRANCA MONTES DE OCA

We are at the point and place where pilgrims used to band together to cross the woods in the wilderness of Oca (it refers both to the river and geese). The woods were rife with all types of thieves and plain bad seeds who robbed, beat, and generally gave the pilgrim a tough and painful time (very much like our modern urban gangs). We are staying tonight in what once was a "hospital" (hostal and health center) that served pilgrims in the 14th century. It has been renovated into a 3 star hotel with a medieval look throughout. Lady Karen of Hoosierdom will seat with me tonight for dinner in the great dinning hall surrounded by flags and shields and a million ghosts. Pilgrims banded together here for the 14 km trek to the refuge built by San Juan de Ortega (disciple of Santo Domingo) in his Church of Saint Nicholas. A detail of the church is the Miracle of Light whereby a beam of sunlight hits the capitel to the left of the altar twice a year during the equinoxes. Women unable to bear children bathed in the light with positive results. A big customer was Queen Isabella who bore 3 children after a pilgrimage to the church and the beam. In gratitude she enlarged the church and had a palio (overhead cover) built over the tomb of San Juan de Ortega. The construction of a road and the presence of Knights Templar and Knights of Santiago did a lot to bring more security to the area (nothing like chain mail and broad swords to put a scare in the ruffian class in any century). Also, near San Juan de Ortega at the western reach of the Montes de Leon lies Atapuerca where in 1994 were found humanoid remains dated 800,000 years old that are currently recognized as the "first European" antecessor to Homo sapiens and Neanderthal. There are also cave paintings in the manner of Altamira and Lescaux. The region had many underground mines that contributed to the findings and now the area is a scientific site designated as "Patrimony of Mankind" by UNESCO. Aren't you glad this blog offers scientific information? We will skip the climb up three hard hills in the Montes de Oca by taking a bus to Burgos. It is one the hardest stages of the Camino and after previous experiences with severe inclined terrain and in deference to the stubborness of the blister complex (uprising is a better word) in my left foot we will observe the Montes from the windows of a nice coach that will deliver us to Burgos in less than 40 minutes and three days before our feet can do it (if they can). Sorry to disappoint the fans but dragging a foot over 3 stages of 12 km each is not a "walk in the park" so we bus that we might walk another day (Besides the fare is about 3 euros). Today's walk was rather easy with a village or hamlet every few km. We did a lot of stops at very appealing benches in shady spots. Seems like the local banks and Catholic Charities are trying to blanket the region with benches. They are a welcome relief in the crossing of a land without shade. We carry about half a gallon of drinking water and Karen delights in refilling our bottles at every potable water fountain (there is one in every village). On top we eat fruit and bread and "bocaditos" of ham and cheese. We stopped at the end of our walk for a victory shanty (beer and lemonade) and marveled at about 15 legs of ham hanging from the ceiling as well as the skill of the bartender in cutting almost transparent slices to make "bocaditos" or trays. Spain is coming increasingly into focus. Hams, stews (cocidos), green salads, red peppers, olives, manchego cheese, lots of young couples, many old women in black and grey, and huge trucks on the highway. On several sections, the Camino crosses highways or runs alongside them. It is like walking along I-69 with less traffic. Usually there is a rail guard. The crossings are signed and there is often a good traffic interval. Traffic police seems to be specially tough.Whenever I might think of wheat in the future, the image of vast acres up and down hills covered with cereal

will always pop in my head with an underlining of poppies. Marvelous, wonderful vistas across valleys and up hills to treed wilderness. Magic. To think that there is in me a trace of people from this region is truly ennobling. I gain no status but add a greater sense of belonging to whatever cultural stew flows within me. Thank you, grandma.

BURGOS

Crossed the Montes de Oca aboard an intermunicipal autobus and arrived at Burgos just at mid-morning. Short walk to one of the historic city gates dating from the medieval times. Then entering the large plaza of the cathedral to become overwhelmed by the concert in stone with a Gothic motif that emerges right before our eyes. Two towers from the 13th and 14th centuries rise to pierce the sky. The first cathedral was built in the 11th century in the Romanesque style of the times but was enlarged in the 13th century and following centuries in the Gothic style with participation of the top architects of the time. In the end the cathedral embodied the best legacies of French, German, and Flemish Gothic design. Along the ambulatory (wide aisle along perimeter of the central nave) there are 17 chapels of various sizes with their own "reredos" or altar pieces carved in wood and richly painted in gold with generous placement of images and relic holders. Some reredos reach 2 or 3 stories in height. The floor layout is in the form of a Latin cross with the tomb of El Cid and Dona Ximena (his wife) at the intersection of the cross. The central nave has at one end a 103 stall semicircular choir and a very large organ. The stalls have carvings of stories from the Old and New testaments as well as the life of saints. On the opposite side it has a 5 story reredos in rich baroque style that truly takes your breath away. The whole cathedral overwhelms the senses. Rich, sensuous, generous display of craftsmanship and faith not only vertical but horizontal as well. It is not just a monumental act of worship but a very large demonstration of civic capacity. We spent three hours at the cathedral and dragged ourselves back to the plaza with an overdose of Gothic. On the way to our hotel we learned of the "fiestas" that start on Friday and will go for two weeks. The old central city area is all dressed up.After a nap we walked to the statue of El Cid but could

barely get there because the bister on my left foot made walking nearly impossible. So, we went to a pharmacy where a very kind lady directed us to the local bus that passes by the hospital. The emergency room accepted us rather quickly, diagnosed our problem, treated the blister with betadine, and recommended three to four days of rest. We are making arrangements to stay at the hotel until Monday or Tuesday and then bus ourselves to Leon with a hoped for healed foot to continue the walk. The blister area needs to stay open with betadine applied periodically. We might after all see the Fiesta de San Pedro celebration in Burgos(at least from the hotel window).

The Arch of Santa María

It was the most important gate to the city throughout the Middle Ages. Till the end of the XVIII century it was also the Town Hall. The principal façade with the shape of an altarpiece was done in 1536 participating in its construction Francisco de Colonia and Juan de Vallejo. The works ended in 1553 with the placing of the statues carved by the sculptor Ochoa de Arteaga and they represent Carlos V, El Cid, Fernán González, Diego Porcelos, Nuño Rasura, Laín Calvo, the guardian angel and the Holly Mary. In the inside, the Sala de la Poridad, the big mural of Count Fernán González painted by Vela Zanetti in 1971 and the Museo de Farmacia all stand out.

Reopened in 1994 as an exhibition hall.

Burgos: Cathedral

BURGOS 2

Rest day for healing of my leftist blister. Just lay about with the foot uncovered and apply betadine. The street below is coming alive for the beginning of the "fiesta" at 6:30 PM today. Ten days filled with activities of all types. There is a Circus in the Plaza Mayor, six days of bullfights with a production of Carmen after that on the last day of the "fiestas", art exhibits, a city wide tapas competiton, concerts, theater, fireworks, parades, dancing in the streets, cattle fair, and all manner of fun things to do for all ages. It will be fun to watch from our third floor window and hopefully from the street with a healing foot. We will be here until next Tuesday (June 29) and then move on to Leon for two days before renewing the march.

Had a long evening after dinner drink with Don Pedro Martin Iglesias in Villafranca Montes de Oca. He took an abandoned ancient hostal and turned into a three star lodging and dinning beautiful place that renders homage to past centuries while celebrating the present and the future. He had to fight preservationists that just wanted a monument with a historical plaque as well as town officials with a narrow interpretation of building and zoning regulations. We talked long about creativity and enterprise with sidetrips to health insurance and medical practice (he is in favor of full coverage without bureaucracy and lawyers). He retired to follow his dream of renovating a historic hostal and shows great pride in telling the story and showing the place. It was a wonderful engagement with the entrepreneurial side of Spain.

Tonight is the first of 7 sessions of the fireworks competition. I will dress my blister to drag my foot to a good chair at a terrace of a bar to watch the show. Love good fireworks. The Chinese were into something great when they invented them (the other uses have not been so great).

Staying put in a hotel room forces a research, writing, and thinking spree. May it be profitable.

Burgos: Plaza Mayor

Burgos; Monument to El Cid

Burgos: Paseo del Espolón

Burgos: Calle Lain Calvo

LEÓN

Jumping from the pot into the fire (or at least the embers). Left Burgos in the middle of its Fiesta of St. Peter ("sampedro") to arrive in Leon at the end of the "sanjuan" (St. John's). A national artisan fair spreads along the streets and the plazas with all manner of handicrafts on display and for sale.

Leon was founded in 68 BC as a Roman legion garrison. A village grew outside the rectangular palisade of the garrison and eventually became a medieval city breaking down some portions of the fence and replacing others with a stone wall. By the 3rd century Leon was the center of commerce and politics in NW Spain. Conquered and destroyed by the Arabs under Almanzor (Big Arab leader of the late 10th century) in 996, the city was later rebuilt and became in the 10th to 12th centuries the capital of the Kingdom of Leon that extended for about half of north central Spain.

The cathedral was built in the 13th and 14th centuries. It is now considered a jewel of early Gothic and is undergoing massive preservation. The European Union has designated it as "patrimony of mankind". It has over 1,900 square meters of stained glass windows. A few blocks north of the catedral is the Royal Basilica of St. Isidoro (a 7th century bishop) built in the 10th century. It is a wonderful example of high Romanesque architecture and art. From time immemorial it has been granted the privilege of showing the eucharist (consecrated communion host) at all times and thus discourages rambling and talking in favor of a prayerful presence that is quite challenging but comforting. A museum next door holds the treasure of the basilica and one can talk at any length. The roof of the basilica has frescoes that predate the Sistine Chapel and are well preserved. Laying on one's back on a pew is a good way to see them instead of risking a neck cramp.

We will explore Leon today and prepare to re-start the walk tomorrow

Burgos: Fiesta   de   San   Pedro (sampedros)

LEÓN 2

A little less populous than Burgos (Leon has about 130,000 inhabitants) it does not quite feel so much, as one walks around. Lots of people everywhere. Often more pedestrians than cars. The center city has a measure of restricted vehicular access. Electronic bollards that look a lot like R2D2 from Star Wars restrict traffic flow for non-permitted users. Underground parking lots at edges of central city help reduce both traffic and parking demand. Pedestrians feel safe and flow in streets all over the central historic area. Somehow, they seem to have discovered that pedestrians rather than cars create commerce. Hmmmm. Elsewhere there are ample (12 feet) sidewalks and well regulated intersections (lights and surface marks) that make walking pleasurable and safe. Sidewalk extensions of bars and restaurants encourage dining and drinking al fresco. It is all delightful.Walked around the oldest section of the city. Time appears to have stopped. Quaint plazas and zig-zagging streets transport us to the Middle Ages. Old chapels and convents along with fountains built by long gone kings seeking divine favor. Hit the Plaza Mayor during farmers market day. Hard to avoid the temptations of fresh fruits. Melons wink at you and cherries sing appeals for tasting and buying. Peaches of all types try to ambush your attention and freshly harvested raspberries, blackberries, and strawberries offer ideas of berry delights. So, tonight there will be a fruit dinner with melon for tomorrow's lunch adding a tasty load to our backpack.Leon's name does not come from lions but rather from a Roman Legion (the VII Legion: Gemina Felix). The name "Legio" was eventually corrupted to "Leon". The Royal Basilica of St. Isidoro hosts the tombs of many kings of Leon (Lion kings? Hakuna matata?) as well as those of other nobles. Just around the corner from our hotel a three story Corinthian column renders an homage of good wishes to some notable in

León: Cathedral

the name of Jupiter. Two storks have built a nest atop the column. When a city has existed for 20 centuries there is much to dig up. Roman ruins connect with remnants of early medieval places that support new developments of later ages. The weather is turning hotter (80 plus degrees) and the forecast calls for things to get warmer. This will make us walk early to avoid the "canicula" or afternoon heat. We should be able to accomplish this. In all cases we will carry enough water and make sure our bodies do not overheat. The change in plans about traveling to Paris rather than Barcelona is now in full swing. We have train tickets and Azu is scouting the apartment rentals in Paris which offer a better deal than a hotel. It will be a wonderful ending to a marvelous adventure. Besides, Azu is expecting our first grandchild.

VIRGEN DEL CAMINO

First product of modernism. The church built in the 60's celebrates concrete and simplicity of adornment with a baroque altar piece. It is more Le Corbusier than a 10th century masterbuilder. The overall effect is the same in that it looks upward with reverence in the language of these times. Heat is increasing and our prime walking time tries to stay in the AM. We got to our hotel at 11:30 after a late breakfast and a walk on hard surfaces from Leon. A great section ran along a large industrial park and very mediocre duplex housing that appears to be a victim of the "crisis" or plain bad design. Saw many Latinamerican immigrants as well as some grafitti and posters declaring "Spain for the Spanish" which contrasts with images of old people pushed in wheelchairs by what appear to be foreign born nannies. Hmmmmm. Big strike and rally later in July organized by a coalition of labor unions and the Communist Party of Spain. Nobody wants to deal with the "crisis" and it is time to vent and blame the rich. Seems like we have seen this movie many times before in the 20th century and there is nothing fresh so far in the 21st century. The script is in Spanish with possible English sub-titles. Yet, most people we talk with appear totally uninterested on politics and very busy with their economics of survival. Had a wonderful chat this morning with a 73 year old woman full of spunk who inquired about our place of origen and proceeded to explain for our American understanding that the current political situation is hopelessly tied in political orthodoxy and upmanship since they are trying to be seen as creators of a "new economy" that blends market economics with socialist fancy in a country of market consumers with a socialist heart. She lectured me high and low on Milton Friedman and how great he was. She had data to back her views and passion to underscore them. Perhaps she is the part of Spain that is fading away or the seed of what is coming. In all, the chat allowed us

to rest in the shade for a while. Our destination emerged soon after at a turn of the street much to our surprise. It might be the same for America (and even BSU). This town hangs on both sides of a regional highway. It has 3,000 people. Both here and in Leon and Logroño we have seen hordes of baby carriages and children under 5 years of age. Looks like bad times have produced a baby boom. Wonder if it is the same in USA. Some of the carriages are quite elaborate and obviously expensive. Baby stores abound. Good thing we are past the baby producing years.We will hurry tomorrow to Villar de Mazarife about 16 km away. Our feet will be up to the challenge after a night of rest in a room without AC but with large windows that allow breezes to flow in. Good thing there is no fiesta hereabouts.

HOSPITAL DE ORBIGO

Well, 26 km in two days. First stage to Villar de Mazarife took us across an oak savannah bereft of shade. Oaks clustered here and there surrounded by grasses. Along the road and probably due to the drainage ditch along the camino there was vegetation similar to a prairie edge (aster, goldenrod, shooting stars, lupines, etc). The major section was sandy dirt with a final 4km approach on asphalt. Temperatures in high 80s to low 90s. We drank a lot of water and probably perspired most of it. The hostel was quite animated and friendly with high marks for comfort.Today's stage of 14.2 km took us on an initial 6 km walk on an asphalt road across fields of corn and sugar beets. Then we were treated to 4 km of a dirt road that could have been an ancient river bed for the amount and size of pebbles. The final arrival section offered a mix of dirt road and city streets paved "Roman style" with stones and pebbles that make walking adventurous unless you are a Roman soldier with thick soled regulation sandals. To crown the day we crossed the Orbigo River (a trout stream) on an old 19 arch Roman bridge now under reconstruction after 20 centuries. Perhaps we need to hire some old Roman bridge masters in our places. During the Middle Ages the bridge served as an honor field for jousts between local knights and their challengers. As we crossed there were several fly fishermen luring the local trout. A famous local dish is trout soup that Karen is not ready to try. The day was hot but we found refuge in a few bars along the way for refreshing pauses. The Spanish bar is a very curious institution. You can get your favorite drink there but you can also get your mail, receive messages, meet your friends to play board games, cards or just chat away the time. You can get a cup of coffee in many ways, eat bread, pastries, or bocadillos (small sandwiches), enjoy tapas all day long or have lunch (12 to 4) or dinner (after 7). You can also read the daily papers (they are always at a corner of the bar) bought by the bar or left by customers. The bar is really a community center very vital to people and place. After about 9.6 km we came this noon to Villavante and spend some time at the local bar receiving a lesson on local history from the barkeep. It happens that once upon a time the town was a dairy and cattle center with a little more than its current 200 residents. A constellation of 7 to 9 small towns of similar size spread over the surrounding country side just about 3 km from each other. Today the cows are gone and cultivation of corn for ethanol and beets for sugar take advantage of large irrigation channels connected to dams and tributaries of the Duero River (major stream in central Spain and Potugal). I took advantage of the irrigation system by dipping my hat in a fountain to cool my head. The barkeep lamented the absence of local food stores. The area baker brings bread and other supplies each morning on a delivery route. Pilgrims and walkers provide additional income by buying food and refreshments at the bar. Rural Spain is slowly been transformed by migration to urban centers and loss of its small villages. We share a similar situation in post-industrial America. Can we find alternatives to entropy? Hmmmmmm . . . Blisters have healed but bodies get tired and the post arrival 2 hour nap has become the custom. Then a shower, some foot massage with special skin softeners and pain killers before walking the town, getting supplies, and dealing with dinner.Only 20 more days to Santiago. Hearts beat in anticipation. We are surrounded with people from many countries and ages intent on the same purpose. Convergence? Just yesterday managed to referee an altercation between three italian walkers and a barkeep. They wanted to eat food they had bought elsewhere in the terrace of his bar-cafe. I had to dust off some Italian to convince them to purchase coffee and then go ahead with eating their goodies. My reward: one bottle of cool water. Let peace reign in the planets. Quite often the camino becomes a

Tower of Babel and there are no referees. People use all manner of gestures to make a point, specially at restaurants. Nosy dabblers in various languages like me can be welcome most of the time. Tomorrow we will have a real challenge with a 16.8 km stage to Astorga (an old Roman camp). It should take us about 5.5 hours or so depending on weather and other factors. We plan on leaving early (7 A.M. or so).

ASTORGA

At the entrance there is a traffic circle that proclaims a welcome to "Asturica Augusta" and then one proceeds to climb the slope to the main street that crosses the historical center. Very soon one sees an excavation of Roman ruins before moving up across a series of plazas to the cathedral square. Astorga dates from the first century AD when a Roman detail guarded the gold mines near the town. It was a crossroads of the Roman world and continued in that role until Visigoth and Arab invaders slowed its progress until the 11th century when it became the juncture point of the French Way (from Roncesvalles) and the Silver Way (from Seville) in the Camino. In the 18th and 19th centuries it became the chocolate center of Spain (it has a Museum of Chocolate) that has vestiges today in the many stores dedicated to manufacturing and selling chocolate products from drinks to bonbons.

The cathedral casts a huge profile upon the city. It is seen from a distance as a dominant form and it is a rather large building with an extensive compound. Across the cathedral sits the Palacio Episcopal designed by Antonin Gaudi before his successful works in Barcelona (Sagrada Familia, Casa Milla, Parque Guell, etc). It reminds one of the castle at Disney World as observed by a Swedish walker.

The walk of 17 plus km was not topographically challenging but it extracted a good deal of sweat and foot power. We made several stops to revitalize our bodies as well as our spirits. The oak savannah of the past two days gives way to oak woodlands and fields of white beets, corn, and hops as one approaches Astorga. Again heat and lack of shade underscore the walk; however, we recovered strength after shower and nap. Our confidence grows.

Tomorrow we will taxi to Molinaseca in order to avoid three hard climbs.

Astorga: Episcopal Palace (Antonin Gaudi)

MOLINASECA

Once upon a time there were grain mills in this place with a nice river and a Roman stone bridge. Those days there are mere memories as the town of about 800 welcomes pilgrims in many refuges and hostals after the hard crossing of several mountains. We are now in what is called "El Bierzo" where Leon fades into Galicia, the last province before Santiago. El Bierzo once belonged to Galicia and was a province on its own but times change, specially over 2,000 years. Chestnuts are blooming in the hills and the terrain is rugged (to use a word other than hard). Spain loves its chestnuts come winter time. We chose to transfer by car from Astorga to Molinaseca in order to avoid the steep climbs and the stiff descents. Our knees and calves are not in mountain condition as we found out in France. It would have taken us more than four days to make the crossing in exhausting journeys of seven to eight hours per day. Mercy!! The goal is to get to Santiago in one piece fully functional in all extremities. If we were 20 years younger this 4 day trek in the mountains would have been an exciting and possible challenge; however, we are 20 years older (not necessarily wiser) and preservation rules over exploration. The car took a route roughly parallel to the Camino and we could see (and feel) the steep nature of the terrain at a speed often no higher than 30 km per hour. Beautiful woods of pine and oak with high brush of various sub-alpine plants leading and blooming yellow to purple down to the valley of the Sil River. The number of pilgrims on the road has increased noticeably. This town has probably 10 refuges that house probably 200 people in various forms of accommodation. The bar terraces are filled with people drinking refreshments or eating "bocadillos" since the "official" dinner hour is 8 PM. Some look quite haggard from several days of mountain hiking. Many move slowly favoring a blister or two while many wear ankle and knee supports. One would think of an army arriving home after a hard fought battle. Tomorrow we will walk about 8 km to Ponferrada. It was a bastion of Templar Knights and Mrs. Cruz is rather excited about visiting the Templar Castle built in the 11th to 12th centuries. Might get myself a coat of mail or tubular helmet.

Molinaseca: Bridge over Meruelo River

PONFERRADA

Ponferrada reflects the request from a cleric in the late 11th century (Bishop Osmundo) to have a bridge built with iron reinforcement (pons = bridge + ferrata = of iron). It is the financial and administrative seat of El Bierzo as well as the residence of most of its population. El Bierzo fits in the NW corner of Leon very much like the tail fits in a hen's outline with the head looking east. The entrance to Ponferrada is dominated by the Templar Castle just as the history of the city has been historically and physically linked to the knights, their deeds, and legacy. We just missed the Templar festival last weekend where the entire town becomes a Templar celebration with the castle at its center. It occurs to us that a bit of "Monty Phyton and the Holy Grail" might possess the entire place. We looked for medieval capes but settled for t-shirts. Of itself the castle is an impressive complex about the size of two football fields on 4 levels. The steps are in the old Roman proportion of about 12" x 12" which makes climbing quite a medieval quest. With temperatures in the mid 90s to low 100s we tried to stay under the shadow of the walls but managed to do just half of the tour in deference to the need for cooling. The Saharan wind system has covered Spain for about one week taking temperatures in the south to the low 100s while the north reaches the mid to upper 90s. We walk until about 1PM at most and then stay low for the rest of the day. Yesterday at Molinaseca our non AC room was uncomfortably hot until a breeze began to cool things off around midnight. Sleeping well gets hard but today we had a recuperating siesta in our AC room before venturing out in the town. Also, the narrow streets offer much welcome shade with additional "pasages" (covered walkways). Such are the trials of high tech Americans in low tech Europe. Pity!! We will do 9 km tomorrow morning trying to avoid the afternoon "canicule" heat stress. On Thursday we need to cover 16 km and a departure at 6AM might not be out of the question. What is really hard is the solar reflection off the pavement that heats up legs, chest, and face. When the feet get hot, the body begins to argue for rest or/and a cool drink. Hope the Saharan system is exhausted soon. One can only drink so many pints of beer shantys (beer and lemonade). It is good to comment that the local basilica holds the statue of Our Lady of the Oak (Nuestra Senora del Encino). It was a wood carved image brought in the 5th century by St Toribio, Bishop of Astorga from Jerusalem, hid from Arab invaders, and found within a tree trunk by Templars while cutting trees for construction timber in 1200. It is the patron saint of the city set in a three story carved wood altar.We are 213 km from Santiago. It is quite incredible.

FUENTESNUEVAS

Like in The Little Shop of Horrors it appears as if Ponferrada grew out of its limits and ate the surrounding communities. Sprawl kills. Good 9 km walk through an endless urban corridor. Rested at two nice parks with lots of shade, people jogging, walking dogs, or just hanging out. Fuentesnuevas was once a little village until the Ponferrada sprawl brought housing, a hospital, and a youth detention (counseling?) center plus more traffic and the extension of municipal transit lines. Cannot see yet if it has been worthy.

A local florist walking with us carrying a basketful of petunias complains of the absence of pedestrian crossings as a sign of something missing in the urban fabric along with a loss of planted medians. "There is a need for a few traffic circles" she affirmed to my incredulous Hoosier ears. Which brings me to civility as a consistent element of the pedestrian-vehicular relationship both in Spain and France. Pedestrian crossings are safe zones respected by drivers at all costs (heavy fines for striking pedestrians). The little green man in street signals offers a safe time for crossings but in other locations it is sufficient to step on the white stripped crossing for traffic to stop. It has taken us awhile to be comfortable with this arrangement. Today, we crossed several four lane streets with ease and safety free from the ire of drivers (there were medians! Not just painted lines). Not just passenger cars but busses and trucks stopped to let us cross. Amazing! Of course, the history of these places has not always been sweetness and joy. From ancient times there have been struggles for dominance driven by greed, hatred, revenge, racism, and other capital and not so capital sinful expressions of humanity. This cauldron has cooked many stews that are now part of history and tend to become some far off Romance. Ponferrada as well as other localities is the product of this. Most certainly, the cycles continue today under different guises. It is good to know them and be aware of their impacts and consequences. The heat is a bit overwhelming.

We stopped at a supermarket and bought fruit, bread, and cheese which we put in our daily backpack hanging from my shoulders. The sun hit my back for the last 3 km and when we took the cheese out at our room it was kind of melted down a bit; so, we enjoyed "melted cheese" sandwiches with a fruit accompaniment for lunch. It is 32 Celsius (89.6 Farenheit) in the shade. Probably higher inside my black shoulder bag. In the Mediterranean coast it is 40 plus (104 F). The air does not move and even dogs just lie down and do not bark as we pass. Tomorrow is a big endurance test for us with 13.2 km to Villafranca del Bierzo. There are no shelters of our predilection along the route and we decided to take the "Nestea plunge" even before the heat wave. We will survive! So, we will get down to basics, open the windows to catch some breeze, watch the Spain-Germany match on TV, and share a melon we bought at the supermarket. Not a bad plan for a hot Summer night in Spain (or anywhere).

VILLAFRANCA DEL BIERZO

Arriving at the far reaches of the Province of Leon before crossing into Galicia reminds us of the "and now for something completely different" skit phrase in the Monty Python show. We are past the "Montes de Leon" and into the "Sierra del Ranadoiro" (Ranadoito Mountains) with a serving of steep inclines before the more friendly terrain. The names of places begin to sound a little like Portuguese but it is Galician along with the food fare. The toughest climb is O Cebreiro that rises 585 meters (1930 feet) in 5 km (3.1 miles) for an 11.7 slope gradient. Some goats might have trouble at this level. The climb is not impossible to do; however, it takes time and for us it might be quite a lot at about 1 km per hour or so. So, this is not the mountain where we choose to die. A taxi will take us tomorrow from Villafranca to Triacastela (138 km from Santiago) to continue our walk on Friday.

Villafranca is an interesting town in that it was established to accommodate Frenchmen who settled here in the 11th century (villa = city/franca = Franks; thus, city of the Franks). It had dual government for some time in deference to French and Spanish residents. This was the "Little Compostela" where pilgrims too sick to continue into Santiago would receive the same pardon given at the Pardon Door of the cathedral in Santiago. Kind of a reprieve after a hard journey. Just like the Holy Door of the cathedral in Santiago is open only on holy years (when the Feast of Santiago falls on a Sunday), the central door of the Church of Santiago in Villafranca is only opened during holy years. As we get closer to Santiago there are more pilgrims on the road. Our refuge is full tonight (30 plus people) and so are other refuges in town. Everywhere we see people with backpacks and walking sticks ambling or resting or taking care of their feet. Knee and foot problems are integral to the Camino experience. We baby our legs and feet with lotions and powders that bring relief to aches and pains as well as building confidence in all things turning out well despite the setbacks. A great number of people go by bike and they have physical as well as mechanical problems. This morning a mother and daughter (Carmen and Mary Carmen) spent some time expressing kindness and encouragement to us. All along the way one hears good wishes and receives affectionate expressions. They are glad for our presence and wish us well as an extension of their own life pilgrimage. To see Karen speak of her life and home in broken Spanish with a 70 something grandmother is truly inspiring. Well, shower time is here. The heat must be conquered somehow.

Sounds. All throughout the Camino there have been sounds. Mostly natural but sometimes mechanical. In France we were enveloped by the incessant chants and pleas of cuckoo birds and doves. In Spain it has been roosters and swallows. Right here in Villafranca has been the torrent of the Arroyo de Pradela (river) just about 30 feet away. It is a rather soothing sound that makes sleep good and restful. We welcomed the sound of rushing and rolling water with a background of rooster songs in the early dawn. The city is all around but river and roosters are determined to make us think of things other than car engines, motorcycles, sirens, loud radios, and other urban annoyances. After a few days of poor sleep on account of heat, last night was a wonderful gift that enabled wonderful rest. Perhaps we will refrain today from looking at the chicken section of the menu. Today shall be observed as Rooster Recognition Day. May our feathered friends go on crowing another day. May the river also keep on flowing and singing its wet and frothy song.

TRIACASTELA

Oak covered slopes all around. This is the small end of the funnel that spouts tired pilgrims for the last 138 or so kms to Santiago. It is different in topography, vegetative cover, and language. While Spanish is the "lingua franca" there is a strong background of Galician that sounds like a bit of Spanish with some Portuguese and dashes of Old Spanish, but it is a language all its own that befuddles many who have managed to get a grip on basic Spanish. Somehow we all manage to communicate.

The autonomous community of Galicia (2.7 million people) is really 4 provinces: A Coruna, Lugo, Ourense, and Pontevedra. The capital is Santiago de Compostela. Galicia proper dates from pre-Roman times with Celts who inhabited the area from 700 BC until the Roman conquest in 135 BC. Moreover, Swabians entered in the 5th century only to be displaced by the Visigoths in the 6th century and then the Arabs in the 8th century. The discovery of the tomb of St. James in the 9th century brought Galicia to prominence and a Kingdom of Galicia emerged in the 10th and 11th centuries only to be assimilated by the kingdoms of Castille and Leon. In all, Galicia has kept its peculiar culture and language often at odds with Christian doctrine and political dominances.A great many Galicians emigrated to South America in the 19th century due to the harsh economic conditions. The land is both beautiful and brutal enabling some agriculture and fishing as major industries. The Xunta (governing body) has done a masterful job of showcasing the Camino as a big financial opportunity. It has built "albergues" (rest hostals) and helped its operators to function and communicate more effectively through the internet. In Triacastela the main street offers about 8 hostals and an equal number of bar-restaurants. Tonight the hostals are full and the restaurants are doing a good business. Beds go for 10 to 12 euros a night and for 10 euros one can have a good dinner with two entrees, dessert, wine, and coffee. Of course, there are also church hostals where the fee is a donation and in some there are sandwiches or soup for dinner. The Camino is a road to recovery for this region. There are also groceries where one can acquire food for the road and essentials like bottled water and Pringles (Karen's happy food).Our walk tomorrow will take us to Pintin (about 10 km away) across soft undulating terrain and through dense oak forests. Our driver today took us along the Camino route through the mountains and our worst fears of inadequacy were confirmed. So, we will fight (walk) another day in friendler territory.

PINTIN

Seems like we are back in France. Dense woods (oak and chestnut) that hide long soft ascents over rocky, irregular, and often slippery ground. The geography will not get you but the geology certainly will try to trip you. Layers of shale and/ or slate in various thicknesses running diagonally across the path or aligned with it. It is often like walking on the edge of a book with randomly spread thickness of pages (fannning from the binder edge). Then water from recent rains as well as Spring fall flows over to make the surface slippery. Suction cups on the soles would have been helpful. Everywhere one can see the usage of shale and slate rock for walls, roofs, shelters, barns, etc. We had a hard but delightful time trying to prevent ankle injuries and admiring the geology with striking colors in ranges of white, gray, blue, ocher, and dark brown.The farm "corredoiras" (alley ways) are wide enough for three people abreast or one cow. On each side there are walls from 3 to 6 feet high. Other Camino sections are wider with great shade that in the fog of mid-morning appear quite foreboding. Galicians inherited from the Celts many notions about (awareness) witchcraft and necromancy that 2,000 years of Christianity has not been able to erase. The dark woods with old oaks and chestnuts of thick, knotty, and twisted trunks in big fern covered grounds are ideal background for fantasies about witches and the dead. Talked to a farmer herding his cows on the Camino. His best cow has given him 4 calves already but her milk is too rich for the making of low fat cheese. He is pondering butchering the cow and getting cattle with lower fat content or watering down the milk. He has made great cheese all of his life and now he does not understand the low calorie fad. "My cow is giving her best" he points out while shrugging his shoulders. Hmmm, we might have to water down design instruction in order to accommodate low calorie course content or make some propitiatory sacrifices. Besides geology, cow sanitary needs cover the path. It keeps one alert. The familiar bovine aroma fills the air like a territorial marking. As we walk, stone steles (bollards) tell the distance in km to Santiago. They are off by 9 km due to rerouting over the years but are helpful answers to the "where are we" question. Our hostel is near the 118 km mark. The distance is an easy 5 day journey for many but we will take 13 days in deference to geography, geology, and personal anatomy (feet and legs) since we want to be graciously ambulatory when we hit Santiago plus there are many things to see and lots of people to engage in conversation.The heat still hangs around but there is more shade. Galicia is very green with hills reminiscent of eastern Ohio or southern Indiana along the Ohio River. Tough to walk but lovely to watch.We will move on tomorrow to Sarria on an easy Sunday 3 hour walk. We will be looking forth to a sojourn at an international hostel.

SARRIA

Relatively short walk with some rough spots. Have come to appreciate natural processes of erosion and water action upon the ground. Exposed layers of shale and other stones often make walking difficult for our cautious approach. Youth and experienced hikers pass us like cars in the autobahn. We are small cars.

Great entry to Main Street via a long stairway to an inclined street. Definitively, Europe is not for the handicapped. No ramps, no special features, no elevators, no concessions of any type. Of course, compassion abounds in speeches and positions but little action in reality. We climb 3 floors to our room. No elevator. Tote your stuff up the stairs. Quite often the steps have no handrail (might destroy the fluidity of the architectural space) or proper landings. Bathrooms have no bars or handicapped toilets. It seems that each one is on its own. Europe seems to be mostly for the young and the able. Is America going the same way? Hmmm.

Cows still rule the countryside in an alliance with sheep. The aromas tell the story. The steps read the witness of their passage. It is usually hard to avoid while doing battle with the geology. Perhaps cows are also affected by geography and geology that causes their digestive systems to evacuate.

Everybody expects the title game of the World Cup and a much desired victory by Spain over Holland. It will be a victory that will solve all problems from economy to politics. A loss will trigger entropy. So much depends on a game played in a politically correct country that will not be able to maintain the large athetic scenaries designed in foolishness to impress the world or enrich the world soccer aristocracy. On Monday South Africa will still be poor and hopeless (few could afford tickets to the games) and Spain will remain on the verge of default with increasing unemployment. Yet, it will play for a mythical championship in a mythical country. Goool!

Tomorrow we will march on for 11 km to Morgade. May the day be cool and cloudy.

Horreo = Galician Granary

MORGADE

Rather comfortable walk of 12.4 km with soft rises and a lot of small villages with cattle farms even at the center. Fresh smell of manure in the air every few sections of road. Shade of oaks and chestnuts that have been along the Camino for many years along with moss covered stone walls. Great walking surface of sand and small gravel that softens the steps and eases the pace. Many refreshment places (bars, fountains, vending oases, benches in the shade, etc) that make the journey more pleasant.

Talked with many walkers who had left Sarria late due to the evening of celebration over Spain's win of the World Cup. Excited about the event but rather cautious about improvements in the economy.

We watched the game until the end of regulation but went to sleep during the extra time only to be awakened by fireworks and car horns. An entire country possessed of sports victory emotion with a rather compelling expression of national unity. The owner of our hostel puts it: "it is about time for us to be one country". The Catalan leaders had planned a large march today to show support for more independence for Catalunya. Seems like it is a bust today (more Spanish flags than Catalan flags showing in Barcelona); but, it will not stop the "nationhood" ambition of the Catalan intelligentsia and its political arm. Along with Catalunya other autonomous communities seek more autonomy led by the ambition and agenda of the Socialist party now in power. Divide and conquer does not appear as a good approach to nation building in Spain and elsewhere. But, what do I know. I am just a non pc professor at a 2nd tier university.

We crossed the 100 km stele just before arriving at our hostel. Due to a measuring error there is another 100 km stele 9 km further up the road. Surveying might not be as exact a discipline as we might think. The earth might shrink and swell from century to century just as temperatures change:)

Tomorrow we march to Portomarin for about 10 km. May the skies remain cloudy.

PORTOMARIN

Last night at Morgade the village population soared to 25 with 20 guests at the hostal. There are more cows than people but all day long pilgrims pass by and stop at the bar-restaurant for food and refreshment. When you turn the corner past a cow barn the terrace with chairs and umbrellas bids you welcome. Twice a day cows pass on their way to the milking barn making a manure trail along their route. It is all part of the environment along with flies. It seems that both France and Spain are very tolerant of flies. No harsh insecticides used around here. Might also be part of the agricultural practice with so many other issues to consider, flies are a minor problem. We just have come to tolerate their presence outdoors and fight them to death in the bedroom. Some of the narrow pathways (correidorias) often have a small creek running on the side or across. Yesterday and this morning we ran into stone bridges either along the creek or down the middle of a small creek.The one along the creek is made of large stone slabs that offer a level surface for 20 to 30 feet. The one in the middle of the creek is made of two narrow slabs of granite about 1 foot by 3 feet each set side by side with water running on both sides. Every few courses there is a cross piece. The surface is rough and the one we encountered this morning was about 600 feet long. Walking on both is safe and delightful. These bridges prevent erosion by water or walker action keeping the road safe and useful while accommodating the water flow from fields and mountains.

Portomarin is a mistake of the great engineering wave in the 1960s. A dam was designed on the River Mino that flooded the existing town that was once one of the most prosperous towns in Galicia. Two churches were moved stone by stone to be rebuilt on higher ground with a "new town" around them. The result is a grid of mediocre buildings along steep streets. As Spain changed after Franco, street names changed and plaques with old names were removed. Somehow new plaques were not installed and locating an address now becomes an exasperating tour de force around town (the tourist office has no local maps). Perhaps erasing the memory of Franco takes time and new street name plaques. After a nice walk on softly undulating terrain, we found the last 3 km quite difficult with a sharp long decline to the reservoir, a crossing over the water on a narrow. 3 feet catwalk along a vehicular two lane bridge. Then one is greeted with about two stories worth of steps that will take you to town. It is design idiocy! Seems that all came out of the mind of a transportation engineer and egomaniac bureaucrats serving a totalitarian regime. Even the 3rd Reich had better design sense! What a wonderful opportunity wasted!.

The relocation of the Church of Saint Nicolas (13th century) served to preserve a wonderful work by a disciple of Master Mateo, one the great cathedral designers of all times.The walk each day is made increasingly more pleasant by the number of bar-restaurants along the route where one can rest and engage other pilgrims in conversation. Also, there are more walkers and the Camino acquires a festive air. We usually leave at 8 am after breakfast. Today we left at 7:30 and had breakfast a few kilometers into the journey at a roadside bar. Yesterday we had come upon a farm woman selling freshly picked raspberries and bought 2 kilos with the intention of having them for desert in the evening. We didn't, and this morning we had them with yogurt at our breakfast place. Wonderful. Some walkers pondered why they had not stopped at the farmhouse with the crude raspberries for sale sign. In late summer there might be a bumper crop of blackberries for all the blooming blackberry plants we have seen along the Camino. Lots of pink flowers as well as small green berries.

Galicia is probably the poorest region in Spain. Great efforts are underway to stimulate tourism as an income generator. It is a beautiful land with very gentle people rich in spirit. Very much worth a look.When you walk in a 6 foot wide "corredeira" with stone walls on each side and a herd of cows comes your way, what do you do?Just step aside and let the cows pass on single file. If you have a stick just wave it and the cow will walk away from you. A short cow shepherd woman taught us this today. Also do not use flash photography in front of the cows since it will startle them with unpredictable results. The shepherd seemed like someone from the land of Oz yet very engaging and proud of her job. We had come a ways down the path and had to backtrack about 30 feet to a wider section to let the cows through a well worn path they have probably used every day for some time.Tomorrow we will do a short 8 km walk to Gonzar on the way to a pair of minor peaks. The weather has become fresher and walking is now less affected by heat.

GONZAR

Walked without a rest stop and found ourselves at Casa Garcia, our hostel for tonight, a bit early (11:30) so we just sat at the bar and sipped cool sodas. Eventually we were led to our room. Marvelous. The government of Galicia in consort with the European Union has made a big investment in rural tourism and hostals along the Camino represent a big boost to local economies. This is a very clean and efficient place that follows on the footsteps of the previous four. Really classy accommodations with shared bathrooms for every two (the social imperative?). No TV in this one but we are tired of the heroic stories from the World Cup champions or Spanish CNN.

Yesterday we stopped for refreshments at one hostel in Mercadoiro half way between Morgade and Portomarin. Fantastic place with a large terrace, tables with umbrellas, extremely clean bathrooms, great bar-restaurant, a garden all around with blooming roses, a fig tree, color everywhere done with elegance, and piped in music that featured Gregorian Chants and Baroque choral pieces. Our 15 minute stop took a little longer than half an hour. It was truly inspiring and relaxing. We also met Zoltan, a Hungarian very keen on knowing about the American Midwest and us. He introduced us later in Portomarin to two Notre Dame graduate students now teaching math and Greek/Latin in high schools at Atlanta and Minnesota.

Galicia is trying hard to present its best face. We are trying hard to hug it with tenderness and euros.This is the fastest we have done a journey but it will not be repeated. There is too much to see and people to meet and talk along the route. Our path today ran through some "corredeiras" but stayed for the most part on forest roads in woods of pine, oak, and cottonwood with a rich understory of ferns and edges of blackberry (zarzamora) and broom. Some Eucaliptus has begun to emerge as indication that we are getting closer to Santiago and its surrounding hills.Gonzar is a small town built almost like a throw of several dice. Streets (better say alleys) run erratically all over the place. At one time they might have been just dirt and gravel but now are paved. One side of town is anchored by a cattle feeding and milking yard with barns and the middle revolves around our hostel and the church/cemetery "complex". New construction peppers the 10 or so homes. With great surprise we were allowed to do laundry in what must be the town washing station right around the corner from the cemetery and about 50 feet from our hostel. Two washing and two drying machines with a large tub of detergent, folding tables and some storage lockers all placed in an open sided stone barn. For the traditionalists or the heavier jobs there was a two people wash tub and a network of clotheslines. Awesome! In most places we either wash in the bathroom sink and hang near the windows or pay 5 to 7 euros for washing with drying on a clothesline. On very rare cases there is a dryer. We carry a bottle of liquid detergent "specially formulated for hand washing with cold water". Tomorrow we will march a little over 10 km on gently rising terrain to Eirexe (Airexe for some). We see Santiago in our hearts.

Zarzamoras = Blackberries in bloom

AIREXE

Wonderful little village at the end of a path that skirts the Sierra of Ligonde (a rough piece of climbing dirt suitable for goats and lizards). We did a competent and rather fast walk along with a couple from the Canary Islands. Of course, the Canaries were not named after little yellow birds but rather after large feral dogs (Latin: can, canis = dog). I even had a banana today from the Canaries that seem to supply Spain with such exotic tropical fruit.At Ligonde, just.9 km from Airexe (eirreche) we met someone from St. Louis who is a good friend of a local WIPB personality (Marcus Jackman) and we spent some time at a barn and hostel enjoying free refreshments from her group (AGAPE) and discussing midwestern things and even things related to Muncie and Ball State. Funny how you travel the world to meet a neighbor next door. AGAPE is the European arm of Campus Crusade.

Our hostess tonight is a very charming and hardworking lady who has built a very comfortable hostel right on the Camino at a point of heavy transit just 71 km from Santiago. This is a rather busy and increasingly crowded section. Many groups have come to the area to do the last stages of the Camino walk and need places to sleep and eat. Our hostel is just rooms and dormitory but across the street there is a restaurant "Conde Waldemar", named after a very famous illusionist of the early 20th century (he was born in Portomarin). The restaurant is also the base for the Galician Fly Fishermen Association that proudly display their trophies and paraphernalia throughout the dining room. Moreover, they have the best pizza we have had in both Spain and France. Tired of the ever present and never changing "pilgrim's menu" we have decided to explore alternatives. Revolutions usually begin at the end of a fork. This all sound like a version of Prairie Home Companion. The weather has turned coldish (upper 60s to mid

70s tonight) but the sun shines brightly in the daytime hours to make us move away from the coolness of the shady side. Hope it keeps like this. Galicia continues to share its green blanket and charm with us at every turn. One Irish travel companion remarked that it looks very much like Ireland. I kind of like that since she also thought that my accent was kind of exotic. Perhaps her Irish brogue and my Latinized English is the point where the world meets.Tomorrow we will walk 10 km to Palas de Rei (Palace of the King) with a small hill to climb and wonderful views to contemplate. Very slowly we are approaching Santiago. We have just learned that the king and queen will be there for the feast. We will be there also holding our "Compostela" or certificate of completion. Somehow we feel awesome although our feet and knees beg to differ.

PALAS DE REI

Galicia is green because of the misty rain that hits its land. Today we celebrated greenery under a persistent drizzle. We had not used our rain ponchos since about six weeks ago in France. The only problem is the steam bath effect under the poncho but as we approached Palas de Rei (Palace of the King or Royal Palace) the water ceased and by the time we reached the hostal the ponchos were dry and folded back in their sacs. Our shirts took longer to dry. In all, this is better than the Saharan heat of one week ago. Santiago, the rainiest city in Spain waits for us just 64 km away.In the rain there was little time to contemplate the landscape but we had the chance to appreciate a rolling land with villages that often ran one into another. Not major centers of population but hamlets of ten to twenty people centered around milk derivatives and vegetable production.

Our double room is a bunk bed with a folding chair and a window to the plaza below. Accommodations and their meaning tend to vary a lot and all looks good over the phone. We took the mattress from the top bunk and set it on the floor to avoid the climbing exercise (experience?). At some point one ceases to be a sprite 10 year old and prefer bedding closer to the floor. Today is one of those times. No chance of finding other places since the town is sold out and the next hostel is about 5 km away. Seems like we are in for a huge crowd in Santiago.

As we walked here there are steles every half and whole km that tell the distance to Santiago as well as information boards. Everybody is well aware of distance left to walk. On many someone has written "casi" above the distance. It means "almost" in Spanish and adds a funny touch to the information as well as a dimension beyond mere agrimensure (distance surveying). The distance is personal and spiritual as well as intellectual and cultural. Santiago is more than a fixed place on the planet. Two nights ago I had a chance to look at the sky. Millions of stars shining above. Kind of overwhelming.

The Camino has often been described as a route under the Milky Way. It is true. The stars line up along its route as if affirming destination and place. Tonight we shall be able to see the Milky Way from our window. What a treat! As we approach the end of the walk the thoughts turn to distance travelled and walked. We travelled about 900 km in France and walked 300 of them. In Spain we would have covered 798 km and walked 300 km. So in total we walked 600 km out of 1698 km (about 1,000 miles). Not bad for two old and out of shape "Americans". Others could do better, we did the best we could and loved every km. The purpose was getting to Santiago in fairly good condition. Mission accomplished (so far). Next Friday we can walk into the city and get the "Compostela" that will testify to our walk. There will be a great fireworks display on the evening of the 24th and festivities on the 25th. Great ending to the journey of a lifetime. Tomorrow we will walk 10 km to O Coto a village of 3 people! It has a hostel named "Die Zwei Deutsche" (The Two Dutchmen) that attracted our attention by reason of its name in the middle of Galicia and Spain.

O COTO

O Coto means "the top" or "the high place". We came to it over a series of hills with strong descents and green tunnels of oaks and eucalyptus along the usual moss covered stone walls. As noted yesterday, more people are now in the Camino with expectation of progressive increase until the 24th. Last night was the kick-off for the "Apostolo 2010" which is the 15 day Feast of Santiago. The big time major feast in Spain. There will be music concerts both profane and sacred along with religious services, parades, exhibits, fireworks, etc. plus our joy in finishing the journey. 63 days of walking and resting. If we had walked the entire distance from Le Puy it would have taken daily journeys of more than 25 km each without rest days and probably little time for sightseeing. We could have increased our walk portion with a few longer journeys but some horses will not drink the water before them and some dogs will not hunt. Within our limits, the walked portion is great and comforting for us alone.

O Coto is listed as a town with 3 inhabitants. It has two hostels and a large car junkyard plus a national road that connects it to Santiago. The pilgrims help the hostels and their bar-restaurants enjoy what can best be described as a "land office business" for lunch (1 to 4) and overnight stays. The prices are lower than farther up the road.We keep meeting again with people we first met a few days ago. It is a wonderful time of re-acquaintance and data sharing. Some have taken detours to sites of interest and a few have walked slower (imagine that!) than us. A lot of young people from Germany, Spain, and Italy now bounce along the road singing or chatting endlessly with that exhuberance of people without great problems and fresh legs. We slugs just stand aside and say "hola, buen camino" (hello, good walk). One sees them later round the hostal or in a plaza filling the air with cheer.Many cyclists also do the Camino.

Some take to the highway while others keep on the path. This morning we saw the remnants of a path/cyclist encounter at a low point where the dirt surfaceOhad turned to muck. Walkers used a stone slab passage but this cyclist tried to cross through the muck. One could see a cycle wheel track suddenly turning into foot prints and splattered muck followed by more erratic footprints and muck droppings on the dry course of the path. It would have been a good scene to film. This could have been the same cyclist who had pushed us aside on his rapid descent. The Camino is just.

As we seat on the terrace of our hostel like a pair of old coots watching cars zip by and hydrangeas bobbing in the breeze, the smell of dinner wafts in. Caldo Gallego will be a first course. It is a soup of collard greens with sliced potatoes that can be both tasty and filling. A second dish will be veal roasted in a wood grill. Dessert will probably be the Tart of Santiago, a sweet almond paste gallette. As usual, there will be wine and coffee. No wonder that weight loss is not a Camino hallmark. We have lost weight through sweat in the walk rather than intake control at the table. However, we have experienced significant appetite loss. We shall see when our bodies meet the bathroom scale in Muncie. It might well be that physical mass has been replaced by spiritual swelling. Hmmmm:) Tomorrow we will do a Sunday stroll of 6 or 7 km to Melide. Two long stages await on Monday and Tuesday.

MELIDE

At 51 km from Santiago, this city of 8,000 is the geographic center of Galicia. It has the oldest "cruzeiro" (stone cross on a column) dating from the 14th century. These "cruzeiros" are set all over Galicia and usually have a crucified relief of Christ on one side and a relief of Mary or a seated, glorified Christ on the other. Usually stand 10 to 12 feet.

Each Sunday until 2 PM there is an open market in several plazas and streets selling clothes, shoes, cheese, vegetables, fruits, etc. plus rides and entertainment.

The short walk from O Coto (6 km) was very pleasant over mostly flat land. Melide is a long city which makes the entry an equally long process. During the walk we have entered many types of cities. Most are set on a promontory for defensive purposes, others are on river edges, and Melide is one now surrounded by industrial and business "parks" of rather sterile design as collaborations between civil engineers, architects, and developing agencies. Their contrast with the old city stock, scale, and layout is quite striking. Next to these "parks" one usually finds new housing stock of utilitarian, boxy, poorly designed type. The late 20th century was not a period of highly creative activity in most architectural practice in Spain and the world. Melide confirms this with emphasis. Somehow the craftmanship of Medieval times makes Modernism seem like an aberration.

Tomorrow and Tuesday we will undertake a pair of relatively long stages (15 km plus) due to the absence of suitable places for overnight stays. The weather forecast is for cloudy days although temperatures should be in the mid 80s. After Wednesday things will be easier with arrival to Santiago on Friday (23rd).

As we get closer to Santiago the mind brings forward the memory of friends who have provided encouragement and affection. They are in thoughts, prayers, and best wishes. Every step has represented a friend and encourager. To all we owe our gratitude and for all we will stand in Santiago. Thank you.

ARZUA

After 15.9 km we dragged into Arzua. It all started on a cool morning with fog still on the hilltops and ended on a long 3 km incline without shade on a hot sidewalk. Somehow the design of entry ways to cities is big on textured pavers but weak on plant material and benches. The guidebooks had forewarned of a series of ascents and descents into 5 river valleys. Good thing there were only five. A couple of ascents led to bar-restaurants that put the spring back on our steps; however, three descents were killers on knees and thighs. Someone had given us a couple of free samples of a gel to soothe bruised bodies. It has a combination of menthol, camphor, gingko, and other "magic" ingredients probably no different to a few over the counter remedies in USA. We massaged ourselves with it after the obligatory hot shower and found great relief. We have other chemical weapons for body soothing but this was most effective despite the strong odor. So, we went to the pharmacy to get a tube. They do not carry it but have some substitutes (pharmacies in Spain and France are funny that way).At O Coto the woman behind the bar commented to me on the softness of Karen's complexion and asked in Galician why had I married an American woman. I answered in my mix of Spanish and Portuguese that seems to approximate Galician something to the effect that she is the most beautiful woman I had ever met. The woman went to the other end of the bar, talked with some women, came back to say "you are very right" and did not charge me for the coffee. Thus, love buys you a cup of coffee and some appreciative looks.

Tomorrow we will only cross two river valleys on our 18.6 km jaunt to Cerceda. For some reason this section of the Camino has a lot of hamlets and towns but no hostels. It is a bit strange since the number of pilgrims increases exponentially from Arzua onward. We are chugging well at 3 km per hour counting refreshment stops. We should be getting to Cerceda around 2 PM to get a good rest for our 6 km stage on Wednesday:)

Arzua is a major cheese making center. Most cheeses come in 2 kilo wheels which is a bit much for us; so, we just order it in sandwiches or omelettes. It has taken us a while to order omelettes or fried eggs since they are usually dry and charred on the edges (grill too hot or too much oil). One gets tired of Serrano (air cured) ham and cheese bocadillos (half a baguette filled lenghtwise with slices of ham and cheese) and have sought to pursue friendly suggestions to amicable cooks who are not inclined to deviate from the prescribed menu offerings. Very few successes but lots of strange looks. When in Rome . . . unless you bring your own kitchen. Last Sunday we discovered deep within ourselves a hunkering for French Toast but settled for coffee, juice, and a croissant. Muncie will satisfy this hunkering in a few weeks.

Melide is the great Spanish center for octopus gastronomie. Karen will not try it but we have come ever so close to touching it at the many "pulperias" (octopus bars) on our walking path and supermarkets. It might be akin to eating bicycle inner tubes but people hereabouts are crazy about it. Perhaps if they hammered it down and breaded it like pork tenderloins. Hmmmm.

We are now 35 km from Santiago. The excitement increases along with the number of people to share it. We arrived at Arzua at 1:30 PM and right now at 7:20 PM there are still pilgrims walking into the city looking for food and shelter. The local shelters have over 200 beds plus those of hostals and shelters. A bed (foam matress) in a shelter can cost nothing (donation) or up to 6 euros with a common shower and services (they are usually at school gyms). Buen Camino, my friends.

CERCEDA (O BREA)

The goal was 18.6 km but we missed a turn and ended adding 2 more km to the journey. Despite all we arrived at 2:30 PM after 6 hours of walking with about 30 minutes of rest/lunch breaks. It is our best effort.

A small blister is trying to emerge on the bottom of my right foot but we will treat it and put it on the healing path. Betadine works wonders.

The announced river valleys were really V shaped and a bit hard on descent and ascent. The dirt and small gravel surface was great as well as the shade from oak and eucaliptus woods. At times it felt like walking through a Vick's Vaporub inhaler. Nice on the lungs!

Many hamlets with narrow corridors (correidoras) zig-zagging behind barns and milking stations. Cows and sheep chewing on fresh feed or grass look at us with a bored look. Guardia Civil (civil protection) on horseback patrol the Camino. We have met them on several days. Makes one feel like a 12th century pilgrim guarded by Templar Knights.

The Camino has become increasingly crowded. At times we walk in a group of 12 or more following and being followed by similar groups. The next three days might seem like a parade. It is really wonderful and makes one walk better and probably a little faster.

Well, it is time to shower, take care of the feet, and visit the bar for a "cana limon" (a draft beer mixed with lemonade).

Tomorrow is a transition stage of 6 km to rest the body and prepare for the two stages into Santiago.

PEDROUZO

Rather than one town we have three small villages come together and accommodate pilgrims. The population is small and the environment is strongly rural. Pedrouzo is the largest and the longest by grace of stretching along a 4-way highway. O Pino and Arca form a triangle with Pedrouzo.

Smooth walk with strong signs of healing for my baby blister on the right foot. Walked with comfort all the 6 km.

Our hostal tonight is part of the rural tourism program. It is an old house (19th century) with a large garden in a small hamlet about 3 km from Pedrouzo. They pick us up and will drop us tomorrow on the Camino. The great great grandchildren have rehabilitated it to its former appearance. Very nice.

Tomorrow we will reach Lavacolla and then Santiago the next day. The air is thick with anticipation by us as well as by our tired bodies. We are ready for some R&R that does not include walking.

The climate is great for plants. Kind of Mediterranean with lots of rainfall. Crocosmia and Buddleia grow to heroic sizes (6 feet plus) and hydrangeas seem to spurt out of thin air with very large pom-poms. It should be a great joy to garden here.

The eucalyptus forest begins to dominate. Some very large specimens with large tracts of younger trees. The air smells great to make the journey quite pleasant. Hope to find more of the same all the way to Santiago. Our lungs will treasure it. Too bad there are no koalas around here.

Yesterday they issued more than 1,300 Compostelas (certificates of completion) at the

Pilgrim's Office in Santiago. That's an awesome number and it will get larger before the weekend. We will be in the middle of it. Perhaps our expectations were too low about the size of this celebration. As we had a late lunch on a cafe by the main road in Pedrouzo we saw a continuous flow of pilgrims. As I said before, this is becoming a parade.

LAVACOLLA

We have come to within 11 km of the cathedral in Santiago. The parade continues. Even little schoolchildren get in the mix. A group of about 30 kids possibly from 4th or 5th grade passed us halfway in this stage. We met them later as they took a refreshment break.The eucalyptus forest with a sprinkling of pines created a mystical environment with a wonderful perfume and great shade. We skirted the Lavacolla airport and never felt the presence of airplanes. Such was the dimension of the vegetative buffer and cover. Perhaps there is a lesson here for buffer design or therapeutic forest walks in urban edges.

For a couple of centuries the Lavacolla River (a narrow creek) was a great must stop for pilgrims. The French monk Aymeric Picaud wrote the "Codex Calixtinus" in the 12th century. Pope Clixto II was initially given authorship thus the "Calixtinus" which has also been known as the Liber Sancti Jacobi (the Book of St. James). It is a five book work that became the guide for medieval pilgrims with description of relics to be found in the various churches, places, peoples, legends, miracles, and hostals. Unfortunately, some errors were made in the translation of names of places from their Latin, Gaul or Celtic roots. So Lavacolla was translated as "wash your tail" or more directly "wash your genitals" rather than "full of stones" from the Gaul: rego dos colos. For many years pilgrims came here to clean themselves before the final walk into Santiago. It was then a good hygienic practice but had nothing to do with the name of the city. It is always good to get a good translation to avoid misunderstandings.So, it also happened at breakfast this morning when a German woman was requesting a shot of hot water to thin her coffee. She used some French in a effort to communicate with the Spanish clerk at the counter but her badly pronounced French was understood as "shot" rather than "chaud eau" (hot water) and the clerk was ready to give her a "shot" of liqueur. With characteristic grace Professor Cruz intervened and made the right translation to the joy of all and exited in triumph to start the daily journey accompanied by the ever beautiful Dona Karen. Hi Yo Silver, away:)

We are spending the afternoon resting and plotting strategy for Santiago. Some cleaning of our sacs is in order to see what do we mail home before going to Paris. Things we have needed in the Camino will not be necessary in Paris.There is much joy in our hearts and minds. This has really been a Magical Mystery Tour that will take some time to digest. Might have even merited a sabbatical leave to create a suitable written and graphic record but my academic peers at BSU have already decided that an effort like this is worthless (or not as worthy as other pursuits more in their dimension). Good thing my family has believed in its benefits and propelled me above the academic fog. People ignorant or unaware of this situation have also provided precious measures of encouragement that have been truly foundational to the success we are already having. The taste so far is wonderfully delicious and like the wine from the many vineyards we crosses, it will only get better with time. Thank you again you all. We will walk into Santiago in your honor and carry on with book and art production with great gratitude to you all. Stay well.

SANTIAGO

Like the Spanish armies in the 13th, 14th, and 15th centuries that cried out "Santiago!" before battle we can now rejoice in saying: Santiago, we are here!

The last 5 km are really a wading through the riff and raff of Modern sprawl. One eventually arrives at the cathedral and its surrounding buildings only to grasp the enormity of the place, the very large scale, and the mind blogging amount of visual stimulation by detail and texture. It is truly a grand site. If the structural components are not enough, there is the ocean of people flowing every which way. Truly, truly awesome.

We arrived, went directly to the "Office of the Pilgrim" to get our "Compostela" or certification of having done the walk. The line extended for about one block and went up to the second floor in a big building of stone and old wood. It took two hours but now we are confirmed as having walked the Camino. Our feet are making sure we remember this. Along with the rest of our bodies.

After getting the "Compostela" we dealt with housing. Our hostel is next to a large park (the Alameda which is Arabic for wooded site) but the street is being dug up for repairs, so we walk through the construction on metal catwalks and a lot of dust. The hostel is in an old historic 4-story house. Very nice.

Just to get ready for Paris we did a cleansing of our backpacks and rushed to the Post Office to mail a box to Muncie. Then we had dinner early and collapsed on our beds for the night victims of over-stimulation and the wear and tear of 63 days on the road. We are in Santiago! Mission accomplished; however, we must see what Santiago has accomplished in us.

We are on line now at 8:45 AM to enter the church and visit the tomb of the apostle that also holds the remains of St. Athanasius. We are just half a block from the door. This will be a madhouse later in the day. It is a jubilee year (July 25th falls on a Sunday) and more pilgrims come.

SANTIAGO 2

From the Plaza del Obradoiro that is on the main facade of the cathedral. We came at 7PM to find a place for the 11:30 show of fireworks and images projected on the facade. The plaza was already full with people claiming about 4 square feet of personal space. More people keep flowing in from the two major entrances. The plaza will be closed at 9 PM. So far, the police has been checking for backpacks that are prohibited. Many altercations and grumblings but full compliance as the men in blue do not cater much to exceptions and nonsense. Really cannot see how the place can hold any more people but there is a full 90 minutes left for the thinnest of human beings can fit in. Beach balls fill the air and food is being consummed. Marvelous sight.

Four great buildings frame the plaza and shade plus a soft breeze give us a pleasant feeling of togetherness. It is kind of a Woodstock festival spirit within a medieval frame. We bought supplies at a market on the way. Water, sandwiches, and potato chips. Have to control the water consumption since no porta-potties are available. This is also a test of biological integrity.

We will talk later about this "experience"

SANTIAGO 3

A marvelous night. Sat for a couple of hours on the stone pavement. Made friendly chat with neighbors who marveled at our trek and very specially the time of "vacation" we had taken. I tried to explain that we are 9 month workers but the concept proved foreign to people on 12 month jobs with benefits and other encumbrances. My right leg went numb and then I tried to get up. Foolish thought. Managed to get on my knees in a space that had been cut in half by a mid-age Spanish hussy and her entourage that dropped almost on my face to take her "space" as has been her custom and probably privilege (Spain is not immune to boorish behavior). She ignored my complaints as well as those of my neighbors to sit among us hearing but not looking in a rather surreal mode and stance. Well, from my knees and a numb leg I tried to stand up and was lifted by a corpulent neighbor who was glad to help the "professor" from America that had come to "experience the best of our country", with emphasis that my unwelcome hussy intruder could certainly hear. Then feeling returned to my leg and it was time to stand for the next two hours until the show started.On the balconies of the surrounding buildings was a display of royalty, government, and upper social castes while we the people frolicked below with song, beach balls, cheers, waves, and social-political chit-chat. The show started at 11:30 as scheduled (color me surprised). Marvelous display of fireworks, music, and multi-media. Truly a magnificent (and costly) production. After the end came the slow exit into the narrow streets. Sardines have more room in their cans! We walked toe to toe all the way to our hostal for a good night sleep that came rather quickly. So was the magic eve of the day of Santiago de Compostela.Over time Saint Iago became Santiago. The Iago comes from the Hebrew Iacov that became the Latin Iacobus, the English James, the French Jacques and so forth. Today we will just rest about. Our plans to attend the Noon high mass have been thwarted by both security and a huge and long line. Local government no longer allows mass entry and over-crowding. Where is the sport on that? The old days of elbowing and suffocating are over. The king and the royals are in attendance. We must behave. Tomorrow we will get up early, don our backpacks, walk a couple of long blocks to the taxi stand, get to the train station, and off to Paris we go.

TRAIN FROM SANTIAGO

Traveling across Spain between Santiago and Hendaye (French border). Scenery we have walked through either physically or closely or from afar. Left at 9:25 and will arrive at 20:40 (8:40 PM) to meet the hotel train at 22:18 (10:18 PM) that will deliver us to Paris at 7:11 AM.

Much more rested. Met two men from Holland and carried on a chat until Leon (6 hours) over a very broad and often deep range of subjects. Managed to solve most international problems and probably start new ones. The financial crisis across the world was foremost but we solved rather quickly by agreeing to tax politicians for 50 percent of income and limiting all to half a term if they plan to run again and one term if they never run again.

Beautiful day. Karen excited about train travel. We passed through some of this land just three weeks ago. The wheat is now ripe and probably ready to harvest. The green is off in the meseta around Leon. In the distance we can see the line of trees that tries to shade the Camino. Memories bloom over the now brown landscape.

Paris will be exciting. We do not want to do the tourist thing and will try to lead a simple domestic life with visits to a few significant locales.

IN FRANCE (AGAIN)

Moving toward Paris in the hotel-train. Our Santiago-Hendaye connection ended with a taxi ride from Irun to Hendaye (5 minutes) due to technical difficulties (line repairs). There was a bus waiting but we were too many and several taxis took the rest of us courtesy of RENFE (Spanish railroads) across the border. Our "sleeperette" seats are fully reclinable and very comfortable. Morning will find us in Paris. The train seems to be packed with people returning from Santiago.

After a "dinner" of Coke and Oreos we will settle for a night's good sleep. The ride from Santiago was quite beautiful and re-affirmed images we had of Spain. The wheat covered hills are now brown with ripe wheat or cropped to stubble after harvest. Some fields even have hay bales already. The sunflowers we saw grwing tall are now in bloom forming great yellow-green mantles next to the wheat. Beautiful sight.

See you in our dreams again with French subtitles.

DERNIER MOTS (LAST WORDS)

There are no words to properly describe the experience of the last 71 days. Incredible, awesome, marvellous, challenging, beautiful come to mind. But also humbling and enlightening along with nurturing and expansive. Perhaps the right words are not the issue but rather the transformative power of engagement with the land, the people, the history, the aeshetics, and the spirit. Just to put things in context we spent the day yesterday at Versailles. It is just 20 km from Paris easily accessed by regional transit. The grounds had free admission and the palace challenged you for 5 euros. We walked the gardens and forsook the palace (Baroque gets to you after a short while). In walking the gardens one is struck by the geometry of hedges and edges in contrast with the wild nature they intend to frame. The intentional play of perspective and focality. The continuous discourse through statuary and fountains about Greek mythology few people today and then truly understood. The play of hierarchy with strong social and political implications. Truly, a challenge to mind and spirit but also a rather banal exercise in grandeur so vast that even the anarchy of the revolution could not destroy. Louis XIV still stands at the gate on his horse proclaiming a victory that cost his grandson (Louis XVI) a head and a kingdom. Yet, the lettering along the front friezes proclaim the dedication of the place to "the glories of France" as if Dalton and Robespierre and the guillotine and the terror had never existed. Such is the irony of history. At the place (Place de la Concorde, once named Place de la Révolution) of massive executions no mention exists of the guillotine or the revolution and an Egyptian obelisk stands by order of an emperor (Louis Philippe) in place of either a pile of heads or statues of revolutionaries. Ironically, official bureaus and agencies fill what once were palaces around the plaza. Yet, at Versailles the display of regal opulence confronts the visitor and confounds the critic as if history never happened. As if everything was merely a dream. Was it? The pathways at Versailles remind us of the Camino with its own irony and force across the land and the people in about 12 regions in 2 countries. A single pathway unifying places and creating a context for a larger story that does not end at Santiago but rather continues in each pilgrim's life. Versailles is a historic reiterative expression of the "glories of France" while the Camino reiterates the permanence of a union beyond the merely physical. Closely cropped and carefully maintained, the green cover of Versailles offers a testimony of craft and permanence as well as inspiration above the mundane. The Camino with its imperfections and physical challenges and incongruencies remains as a place for individual victories in a vast natural and spiritual context. We finished. We won. Yet, we do not really know the end and the prize remains to be claimed. Thank you again for support and prayers.